The Power of Hope

THE ONE ESSENTIAL OF LIFE AND LOVE

ﻫ

MAURICE LAMM

RAWSON ASSOCIATES
New York

RAWSON ASSOCIATES
SCRIBNER
Simon & Schuster Inc.
1230 Avenue of the Americas
New York, NY 10020

Manufactured in the United States of America

1   3   5   7   9   10   8   6   4   2

Library of Congress Cataloging-in-Publication Data
Lamm, Maurice.
The power of hope : the one essential of life and love / Maurice Lamm.
p.   cm.
1. Hope—Religious aspects—Judaism.   2. Judaism—Psychology.
3. Self-help techniques.   I. Title.
BM645.H64L36   1995   95-20249
170'.44—dc20   CIP

ISBN: 0-684-81228-2

All quotes on opening pages of chapters not attributed to other sources
are the work of the author.

Contents

༄

CONTENTS

Acknowledgments

ᔰ

A few close people were very important to me in writing this book and in sustaining my own hope in my Hope Project, and I thank them.

Michael Medved, noted theater critic and good friend, who gave me the initial push that propelled me from the starting line on this project.

My wife Shirley, who deserves a medal for her unflagging encouragement. She was, and is, the power of my hope. She sustained me when I was skirting the shadows in the valley.

My brother Norman, who has been my lifetime adviser, confidant, and best friend.

A·l·a·n A·l·d·a is a star—of acting, writing, and directing. But more than this, he is a star of humaneness, and his advice on this project was enormously helpful.

Eleanor Rawson, my publisher, who demonstrated patience and confidence in this project; Leonard Korobkin, for his friendship, his generous spirit, and his always sage legal advice; and Mel Berger, my agent at

ACKNOWLEDGMENTS

William Morris, who saw the value of this book from the very beginning.

I have had no formal teachers in this rarely analyzed subject, but a number of intellectual giants, aside from the prophets and sages, have helped shape my view of it. These writers form my "ghost faculty," as Max Lerner called it. They are scholars of hope, and include Karl Menninger, Norman Cousins, Paul Tillich, Jerome Frank, and Ernst Bloch; and living eminences like Herman Feifel, Erich Cassel, Leon Kass, and Bernie Siegel.

More than all else, I thank God for enabling me to serve human beings with my meager talents.

The Power
of Hope

Before You Begin This Book

Hope injects tension into our beings—the tension of the bow that stretches to propel the arrow. The tenser the string, the more powerful the shot.

ε&

WHAT IS THIS THING CALLED HOPE?

We know in our bones that hope is every-thing. In the back of our minds we suspect that it is nothing at all.

Like the bond in good paper, hope is the watermark that is found in the very texture of the human condition itself. Think of it: The word *hope* slips unnoticed into our speech whenever we make a judgment, in virtually every hour, every day. It is used so often it has become a mindless, throwaway truism.

The idea of hope is so pervasive that poets in every age rhapsodize over it, and the psalmist writes about it in every chapter of Psalms. Alexander Pope expresses the sentiment of every disheartened person who has squeezed through a crisis: "Hope springs eternal in the human breast." It doesn't only spring eternal, it springs universal.

Dante taught that not until we reach the outskirts of Hell are we divested of this most precious of all human

15

faculties: "Abandon every hope, ye who enter here." Hopelessness is Hell. But humanity could not bear to be deprived of hope even then. Jewish mystics taught that also in Hell there is hope: The soul could take leave of Hell every week—to celebrate the Sabbath!

In Greek mythology, Pandora, the first mortal woman, received from Zeus, king of the gods, a strongbox that she was forbidden to open. But the temptation became too great—and she opened it. Its contents? All human blessings. Reveling in their freedom, all but one escaped and were lost. The one that remained was hope.

This is one essential blessing that has remained in mankind's grasp. Many other blessings could vanish, but without hope humanity could not survive.

The human being cannot even imagine living without hope, because it is like living without a major dimension of life. It is unthinkable, because our whole being is shaped by a succession of hopes. We simply could not bear the terrors of the mythical night without knowing, in the subvaults of our souls, that dawn is just over the horizon. How, we wonder, did Adam ever survive the first twilight on earth? To lose hope is to lose life.

The problem is that everyone talks about hope but no one has pinned down exactly what it is. The poets embrace it, but the scholars by and large haven't touched it—until recently. Why? Because they assume hope is feather light, airy, playful; not something weighty enough for scholars to examine. They cede it to preachers and demagogues. After all, it is based on anecdote; it doesn't lend itself to scientific analysis; it is not capable of being proved; it is not based on reason. If it is beyond reason, some folks deduce, it must be an illusion.

In terms of strict logic, writing it off as just an illusion might be plausible.

But there is this predicament: If it is sheer fantasy, *why is it that no serious person can live through tomorrow without it?* Ask yourself: How come everyone you know has this innate sense of hope, which is a part of everyone's constitution, an essential element that defines our humanity, that enables us to look ahead to tomorrow, to next year, to retirement, even to beyond the grave?

Researchers discovered after World War II that American prisoners of war who were convinced they would come out alive and who had an assured belief in their futures on the whole emerged with less psychic damage than those who felt they would never come home.

Simply stated, those who have no hope at all are nowhere to be found. They are paralyzed by deep depression, at home or in an institution, or they have taken their own lives. Dr. Edwin Schneidman at the University of California at Los Angeles has demonstrated conclusively that hopelessness is the most dominant feature of those who commit suicide. Without at least a modicum of hope there is no use in living. Dr. Elisabeth Kübler-Ross has shown that even terminally ill patients are generally more hopeful than suicidal people.

Hope Is a Mystery

Think of it: Without hope, no child could emerge from helpless infancy. Without hope, no person has a future. Without hope, no society could survive. Without hope, there is no religion, no community, no friendship, no achievement, no country. Without hope, life is a meaningless and absurd existence. Without it there can be no love and no family life, because no marriage can survive hopelessness. Everyone needs to face the fact that life holds more despair than pleasure, and without hope, we could not live our lives through.

For all that, hope remains an obscure faculty of the human being.

Hope is a paradox. It's up in the air, yet it is ground zero. You can't go to the bank with it, but you can't leave home without it. You can't marry without it, you shouldn't go into business without it, you can't start a research project without it, and you can't raise a child in this world without it. Unquestionably, without it there is little incentive to live at all. On the other hand, you can't base a marriage on it alone, and your business needs a whole lot more than hope.

Hope is not only a paradox, it is positively mercurial. It changes from person to person, and society to society; even within individuals and within societies. Hope reformulates itself spontaneously in response to external conditions and internal fears. It enlarges when the news is good, and diminishes after even a small blow to the ego.

Its profound complexity belies its surface simplicity. Religious leaders have consistently used hope to buoy the spirits of their flock. But demagogues have utilized it for their own nefarious purposes; quacks have bottled counterfeit hope for a quick sale; and politicians have used it to cover up their mistakes.

How can we detect the wrong use of hope? Dysfunctional hope obstructs personal therapy and social progress; false hope makes many people vulnerable to charlatans and hucksters; and passive hope is often not hope at all, but a smoke screen to conceal resignation from life, or surrender to what we hate.

Yet we have not isolated it in laboratories, or defined it, or measured it, and we do not understand it. Why haven't we learned more about legitimate hope, if it is so all-pervasive, so ever-present, so critically needed? Obviously, society has not developed a healthy use of hope to remedy its many ills.

Hope Has Spectacular Power

But we now know that hope can motivate us to grow beyond the ghetto. It can make us better suited for our own promotion. It can make us better able to manage daily stresses and setbacks. It can help us ride out severe personal crises and cope with critical illness. It can even enable us to enhance the way we handle our own aging, and to be more satisfied with life.

Hope is very much a contribution of God to humanity. Religious optimism is a buoyant, irrepressible, unflagging self-confidence born of hope—an indefinable, unreasoned, logic-defying expectation of delivery from the most horrendous circumstances. If we don't use it we are ignoring a gift that is as free as our minds and our imaginations. The spiritual quality of our hope can enable us to grow personally, to look with optimism at the future, to broaden our horizons, to dream the dreams that make people great. How can we make the transcendent connection that can open the spigot of hope inside us?

Hope contains spectacular power, as though it captured bits of the bursting energy of creation. Psychologists at major universities are now discovering that hope is more potent than anyone had expected, and that it plays a significant role in a wide variety of human endeavors—in school, on the job, and in the family.

Hope also provides measurable advantage in regard to our health and in all forms of depression.

Psychiatrist Dr. Flanders Dunbar was cited in *The Christian Herald* as having had two cardiovascular patients who were equally ill. One said, "It's up to you now, doctor." The other said, "*I've* got to do something to get me well." The first died; the second recovered. How can we penetrate the mystery of hope, and how can we harness its might to help us cope with our troubles?

What We Need to Do

This is the difficult task we tackle: to materialize hope and to give it shape, to take a sensation and make it into a structure. We need to analyze what hope is capable of doing, extract it from the entanglement of cobwebbed daydreams, raise it up from romantic wishing wells, and then distill it for our own purpose, and use it to help humankind.

We need to learn where it originated; how we should apply it; how we can tell when it is dysfunctional; how we can help generate its power when we find it deficient in a person (including ourselves); and how we can open up our spiritual connections, whatever our religious belief, to validate our deepest hopes.

And we need to design a Hope Therapy to help those

who are depressed as a result of a shrinking vision of the future, rather than from a warping of the past.

These are the areas of hope we must probe through the insight of tormented Job; the intelligence of philosophers; the penetrating intuition of prophets; the flight of mystics; the maps of poets and the anecdotes of wise old people; and through story and parable and metaphor, and the jewels of biblical narrative.

We need to be wise in our handling of hope, as much as we need to be smart in our managing of reality.

CHAPTER ONE

Looking for People Who Live on Hope? Look Around You

> Hope is natural. We all possess it. It needs only to be *un*covered, not *dis*covered.
>
> ❧

T ake my hand," I say.

She does. You see, we have come all the way together. It is an afternoon in March, in 1993, and my wife Shirley and I are walking side by side through the Hartsfield International Airport in Atlanta, Georgia. Around us, in the huge cavernous space, life is exploding everywhere.

The passenger terminal is the largest in the world, covering fifty acres and accommodating fifty million people every year. The parking lot outside holds close to twenty thousand cars. Thirty-seven thousand people work here. Nearly sixty thousand air carriers come and go each month, with four million passengers.

We know none of this. We only know that we are a little band of people clustered here—Shirley and me, our daughter Judith, her husband, and their seven children, our grandchildren—suffused with great joy and with a sense of deliverance. It has been a rough trail and a long year, but our dreams have come true, and the hope we never lost in the worst of times has now turned into reality.

I have been an ordained rabbi for thirty-eight years. From the beginning I have tried to help as many people as I could, to counsel each according to his own loss, her own crisis, her particular heartache. I had to learn how to do it.

No rabbi, or any other clergyman, is automatically equipped with all the answers to the problems of the human heart. You pick it up as you go along, and if you are like me, you often feel that you do that very slowly. As the years passed, however, I began to notice a single unique factor in all my counseling—the anguish I heard had many sources; obliterating it had only one. Very early on I copied a definition of it from the New World Dictionary: A feeling that what is wanted will happen; desire accompanied by expectation. To want and expect; to trust and rely.

I still keep it on my desk. It is a definition of hope.

As I mentioned, when Pandora, in Greek mythology, opened her golden box and all the blessings of man escaped, the only thing remaining was the iridescent jewel called hope. That jewel belongs to all of us; I learned to use it and I am going to tell you how. You see, when I discovered it for myself, I discovered, too, that people don't know *how* to hope. *They really do not know.* Or, if once they did, it is a gift they have lost in the disequilibrium of daily living.

This is not a flight of fancy that will disappear from

sight at any minute. This is a ten-point plan that I have perfected. If you follow it precisely, your dreams can more plausibly come true. It works. It is not magic. It is not hocus-pocus. It will be of the utmost help, of course, if God is on your side (and you on His) as you move along—but, then, would you want Him anywhere else?

On that April afternoon in the airport in Atlanta, in a very personal way it happened to me. I saw the power of hope, the resiliency of the dreams it gives us, the way any one of us can harness it and make our aspirations more than idle wishes. Let me tell you about it.

My daughter Judith, who is thirty-five years old today, was seventeen when she was diagnosed as having Hodgkin's disease. She had graduated from high school and gone to Jerusalem for a year of study. She was intense, alive, and single-minded in her ambition: she wanted to teach Judaism to adolescents. Three months after her arrival, while fastening a string of pearls, she noticed a lump on her neck. In her next telephone call she mentioned this to us, and we insisted she fly home to Los Angeles and have it examined by doctors we knew and who were our friends. But friendship cannot change biology. The lump proved to be a tumor that was malignant and was metastasizing. There were tests and more tests, lymph angiograms, and bone marrow tests, but in the end the verdict was the same—Judith had Hodgkin's disease.

We were devastated; I was furious at the injustice of it all; my wife Shirley was heartbroken. At one point Shirley slipped away from me and I found her in our bedroom hugging the bedpost and sobbing. Both of us fought our demons, both of us were overwhelmed, but through it all, we never believed that Judith would die.

By then I had already been focusing my preaching on the power of hope for several years, but never before had it been so intensely personal. It had never been close to home and I had never realized how all-encompassing it is. As the days passed, I found out. I didn't hope for life for Judith; I found I hoped for the return of her spirit. I hoped she would marry. I hoped she would have children. My hopes kept rising higher. Through all the pain and the crying, the weakness and the appetite loss, the radiation and its aftereffects, my hopes always stayed steps ahead. When the radiation proved successful, the doctors announced that as insurance for her recovery they were going to begin a five-month period of chemotherapy.

All right, Judith said, if they must, they must. But it would have to be done in Jerusalem. She was going back no matter what. How can you let a sick child travel ten thousand miles away from you? Well, hope means stretching beyond your reach. And, perhaps almost instinctively, we had given hope to Judith when we brought her home—we had bought her a round-trip ticket. That return ticket was now her passport to the future.

She flew back to Jerusalem and, almost immediately, there was another crisis. She had a strong adverse reaction to the chemotherapy and was rushed to the hospital there, where, because of crowded conditions, she had only a bed in a hallway. When I learned this, my guilt and rage shook me to my roots. I might have been crushed by my anger but for the strength of my wife. *She will be well. Period,* she said.

With that, Shirley descended on the airport in Los Angeles; browbeat ticket agents; shuffled reservations, seats, and routes like a circus act; and, with our daughter Dodi for company, completed the travel arrangements and reached Judith's side the next day. Was her assurance a mother's instinct? I wondered. Whatever it was, I believed her. I prayed for her and I prayed for Judith.

Wise men say that a person who prays for others is healed himself. That is what happened to me. I consciously hoped and I never lost it after that. I held on to it for five years as Judith was recovering, until she was well again, bright and beaming and crazy and beautiful as ever. When she was twenty-four she married and began creating a marvelous family. Shirley and I believed then that all our dreams for her had come true. I was confident, maybe even smug, in talking for years about my daughter, the survivor. Then it struck.

Judith and her family were living in Atlanta, and she was expecting her seventh child. Shirley and I talked with her often on the telephone. In conversations we had during what proved to be the last days of her pregnancy, we began to notice that her voice sounded worse with each call. It was not the voice we knew. It was growing weaker every time we talked, and it was accompanied by a persistent cough. Her internist had diagnosed a mild case of pneumonia. The baby, our granddaughter Penina, was born prematurely. After that, Judith only grew worse. At last we could stand it no longer. "Sometimes parents, not doctors, need to decide," Shirley said. She convinced Judith to fly to California, met her at the airport, and drove her directly to a throat specialist.

A battery of tests was performed that day, and the next morning the diagnosis came: a massive malignant tumor directly behind her heart and larger than her heart. It was pressing on one of her vocal cords, the reason for her distorted voice. Her condition was considered far more serious than it had been the first time, for this was a remnant of the original malignancy that had never been eradicated. Recurrent Hodgkin's.

The first time the power of hope had nurtured us— we believed and our hopes had been realized. Now more than ever, we needed it. A second occurrence is far more dangerous. But we were older, more mature, more self-confident, and more experienced. We would study every medical option. The medical facts we did not have at our fingertips we would learn; we would take nothing for granted. We would leave nothing in other hands. If we had to, we would alter our lives to solve our problem. And we would win. Again.

JUDITH

The first time was so different. I was just seventeen—when you are seventeen you feel immortal. Nothing can happen to you. Even when you find that something has happened, after you sit in the living room and cry for a while, you stop and you convince yourself that, no matter what, you can beat it. Some people say there is no such thing as a woman's intuition, but there is. I had mine, and it told me I had a future. With God's help I was going to make it and I was going to make my life better. If you have hope that is as real as the one I had, you can make what you hope for happen. It did. I got better and my life went back on course.

When I was twenty-three, my former high school principal introduced me to a man he thought I might like. That was an understatement. I married him when I was twenty-four, and today we have seven children, two boys and five girls. My seventh child,

Penina, was premature. She needed a shunt implantation, and instead of coming home with me, she was placed in the intensive care unit at the hospital in Atlanta.

Then, a month after she was born, the cancer returned. I have some feeling that her premature birth may have been triggered by the onset of my illness, but I have no way of knowing this for sure. In any event, this time I was not responsible for only myself. I had seven children to care for and love and raise to be good people. The oldest was only eight. But I knew I would be able to do it—I just knew it. I believed with certainty that I would recover—I never for one moment gave any thought to the possibility that I would not. God must have had his reasons for bringing the illness back, but now that it had returned, He was there to help me defeat it again as well. Hope does not mean dreaming on about the future. Hope means aiming at it and just refusing to believe that you cannot make it.

At the time, my husband was a school principal in Atlanta and our three oldest children were in school there. We decided to leave them with their father and to leave the newborn, who was tethered to an apnea monitor, in the hospital there, too. The three smaller children and I went to live with my parents, who rented a temporary home near the cancer center in

Los Angeles. The long process of getting me better, and keeping us together as a family all the while, began with fear and trembling—and hope.

I had a great new tool with which to keep my family together—a fax machine. The children in Atlanta sent me their homework and messages, and I sent messages back to them. They sent me pictures that I focused on during chemo sessions, and every two months they flew to Los Angeles with their father for a visit. That was a lifeline for us all. Meanwhile, at my parents' house, on afternoons when I felt well enough, my mother and I went to a nearby toy store and stocked up on surprises to give the little ones, to let them know that I was there for them, even though I was in my bedroom behind a closed door much of the time.

I was a captive of the chemicals in my therapy. This lasted for nine months—and it was a very long nine months, but I never gave up hope. Never. I just knew it would be all right. We all knew.

Today I keep a box on my night table that I call my miracle box. It holds mementos, little things I collected in those days when I was waiting for the next miracle to happen. Every day I sewed the costumes that my children, husband, and I were going to wear on Purim, a Jewish masquerade holiday. It was my hope in action. Sure enough, one week after

I returned, we piled into our van—me as Snow White, and the seven children as the Seven Dwarfs—and stopped at our friends' houses to bring food and say, "Happy Purim, we're back!"

SHIRLEY

It was a long nine months. My husband and I are not that young to have babies in the house. I hired a housekeeper to help, in part because I was taking Judith to the cancer center almost every day. This was the hardest part of all—keeping a smile on your face when you wanted to scream, always keeping one eye on Judith and one eye on the pre-meds and chemos to make sure they were dripping properly, and never showing alarm when blood counts went down or temperature went up. I had a feeling that if I kept calm, Judith would use my face as a barometer that everything was okay and that she would make it. After each session she was so very ill. In a single month, if we were very lucky, there might be three or four days when she felt a little better—that's when we made our trips to the toy store to send gifts back home.

I never let the little ones see how really pained and perplexed she was. I would throw myself in front of her if I had to, hiding her from them, and I would ask my husband to take them for a walk. I wanted them always to know that it would be all right. I didn't let Judith give in, either, no matter how sick she was. Not all the way. I refused to let her leave the house, even in her worst moments, looking frumpy. I believe in dressing up when you feel down—that alone gives you hope. It shows everyone you meet that you are not out, you are only stalled—soon you will be up and blooming again.

There is a gift shop at the cancer center and every week, without fail, I took her there and bought her a gift. Sometimes it was a long, long walk—too long, she complained, but I made her do it. I was sure the presents she could hold to her heart would diffuse the toxins injected into her arm. It was an aggressive strategy that spoke clearly of hope. Judith and I even struggled with ceramics. She is gifted and very creative. We spent evenings creating presents for all the holidays ahead—Mother's Day, engagements, birthdays, all of them. It was our way of showing that the way to shore up our hope was not to think about the pain, but to practice for the future. It diverted us both and it turned our thoughts to family obligations. In the midst of a disease it was a healthy place for our thoughts to be.

WE MANAGED

We learned to be careful with words. We could never fully answer the question "How is she?" with anything other than "Fine." We knew that "Fine" is inadequate to those who are seriously concerned—although we could have better answered "How is she *today*?" To do that, though, we would have had to recite a litany that would depress people and confirm us as miserable victims. No matter what people say about wanting to be told the truth and feeling compassion, most of them are quickly overcome with compassion fatigue and simply cannot take bad news. They need *you* to buoy *them* up. They can't stand groaners. They will deny it, but people like you more when you suffer less!

We told the facts in detail only to close relatives and intimate friends. To everyone else we ended every answer with a note of hope, "We expect she's going to do well," which elicited "Oh, I'm so happy to hear that." Or we said, "It's better than it was last week," and we got back, "That's great. I hope she keeps it up." This happened daily. We agreed that we could say whatever we wished, so long as we ended on a note of hope. And every time we did that we experienced hope deep inside ourselves.

If you are at a party where everyone drives and alcohol is being served, you know that the thing to do is to designate one person per group who will not drink and who will do the driving. This is just the way we handled Judith's illness. Judith needed someone to listen to her, to advise, encourage, and drive her forward: Shirley was our designated driver. She was indispensable for being not merely supportive, but actually supporting.

All our days were busy and I had little time even to think about the gravity of our situation. In the middle of the night, though, when darkness was all about, we would be gripped by dread. Our fears rose up then, with questions to which I had no answers. Perhaps it is a case of "Physician, heal thyself," but none of us is immune to this kind of terror. I had to turn on all the lights in our living room to unsheathe the night of its mystery. I would walk back and forth and talk to God man to man.

Our prayers were answered, our hopes realized. Judith lives in an age of miracles. Discoveries are made every day; research is profound, innovative, and far-reaching. Behind all this there is, of course, the One and Only whom I always have trusted the most—God.

Judith:

> *I asked God what I could do in return for my life, and I honestly believe He gave me a message. I chose twenty-five people, almost at random, and I set out to show them just who God is. When I was finished, I had twenty-five fervent believers. "Keep me around, God," I said, "I'm good for you!"*

And so there we were in the airport, all laughing and crying at once, all celebrating the fact that on that March afternoon, Judith had come home. Two of her daughters had returned a month earlier, so there were six children waiting for her at the gate. It was pandemonium, but a pandemonium of joy. Children were jumping up and down and swarming about the frail but radiant figure of their mother. Perfect strangers stopped and stared at this incredible outpouring of delight. Anyone would think something wonderful had happened: Well, something wonderful had! A few people even cheered and a few congratulated us—for they knew not what.

At last Judith surveyed the scene, stood up, and spoke. "Okay, troops," she said. "Stand tall and move out!" Nobody hesitated, nobody paused for a moment— Judith was a mother again. This is what a dream come true is all about—when the life you long for is yours to live once more. They marched out of the airport and headed home.

Everyday Hopes for Everyday People

ﾞ➋

- I hope I see each day as a brand-new challenge. *I hope I never wake up saying I'm tired.*
- I hope I'll never be content just to pass: *I hope I'll aim for the highest marks in the class.*
- I hope I can tempt fate, nod, seduce it, and win—*but that I never blame God if I lose.*
- I hope I have good luck in life—*but that I not depend on it.*
- I hope I'll always be the little engine that could. *I hope I never ever learn the word* can't.

CHAPTER TWO

Are You Afraid of Hope?

Elie Wiesel, the Nobel Prize–winning author, came upon a remarkable find in Breslov, Poland. Over the entrance to the oldest synagogue in the city, he discovered a sign that had uplifted the ghetto dwellers 150 years ago. The simple words of this lasting sign became an immortal moral challenge many years later during the Holocaust, when no future at all was discernible to its potential victims. It was a compelling cry:

GEVALT! DON'T GIVE UP!

"Gevalt" is "Woe!" Do not submit. Gevalt! Fight back.

કર

Whether we admit it or not, many of us are afraid to hope—and we are afraid *of* hope as well. Maybe we equate it with taking a chance, with the long shot, with reckless gambling on the future. Risk-taking may be so contrary to the Puritan ethic by which we are raised that we are embarrassed even to admit to anyone that what we have to depend upon in the conduct of our life is hope—as if it were some will-o'-the-wisp and more sensible people would give short shrift to it. The fact is, hope is none of these. Hope *is* our future. It is our big chance. It is where our true love lies.

David Mahoney, in *Confessions of a Street-Smart Manager*, illustrates what I mean. He was one of the corporate stars of the eighties—among other things, CEO of Norton Simon and the first CEO in American business history to draw a million-dollar salary. He came up the hard way and formulated his own strategies for success. Here he gives an example of how he learned a lesson in hope:

My wife and I were in Fort Lauderdale, Florida, vacationing with another couple and I chartered a cabin cruiser, a forty-foot Chris-Craft. My boating experience was limited but good enough for cruising about. Then I got an idea.

"Let's take a cruise over to Bimini in the Bahamas," I suggested. "It's only a few hours away."

"We'll be out of sight of land," my wife said. "How do you know you can find Bimini? It's only a speck on the map."

"It doesn't sound like a good idea to me," said my friend. "If we miss the Bahamas we'll be out in the South Atlantic, with Africa as the next landfall."

His wife agreed. "I'd just as soon not end this delightful vacation by being lost at sea," she said.

All this shook my confidence. Maybe they were right. I wasn't familiar with this particular boat and I certainly wasn't a professional navigator. Maybe it wasn't such a hot idea. Still I couldn't let go of it.

I decided to do what I always do when faced with uncertainty—get a professional opinion. I set out down the pier looking for help. Finally I found a wiry character sitting in the cockpit of his deep-sea fishing vessel. With a captain's cap pushed back on his head. He was viewing the passing scene with what appeared to be philosophical bemusement. Experience at sea was written all over him.

"Mind if I come aboard?" I asked.

He nodded, his clear eyes taking my measure. I could see that my credentials as a captain of industry would carry no weight with him.

"I need some advice," I said. "I want to cruise over to Bimini but I've never done it before. My wife and friends are afraid we might get lost. Frankly, I'm a bit in doubt myself. I might have trouble finding Bimini, and if I miss it there's no telling where we'd end up."

Without changing his position the captain said, "How much fuel does your boat carry?"

I told him we carried fuel for about ten hours at cruising speed.

"Do you know how to do a one-eighty?"

He said, "You know the difference between having the sun in your face and the sun on your back?"

I said I did.

He said, "You haven't got a problem. You cruise toward Bimini for four hours. If you don't hit it, you do a one-eighty and cruise in the opposite direction. By then it will be afternoon. You'll know you are heading in a safe direction because the sun will be in your face. There ain't no way you can miss the coast of Florida."

I felt somewhat humbled by this reasonable logic.

When I shared this newfound wisdom with my wife and friends, their hesitancy melted as quickly as had mine. We left the next morning, hit the Bimini harbor on the nose and on schedule, had a wonderful time, and, as the skipper had predicted, had no trouble finding the east coast of Florida on the way back.

I have thought about that old salt many times, especially when faced with new situations where I have felt handicapped by limited experience or information. He made me realize that the tendency often is to focus on the risks of a new situation when the risks may actually be a lot less than you think.

The old fishing captain taught me one thing: Trust your hopes, not your fears.

Generally, we are afraid of hope for three main reasons: First, *hope seems so fanciful; fear so logical and persuasive.* This is just not true, or, at the very least, it is overstated. No, hope is not a science, and no, it is not bound by the rules of logic, and yes, it can jump the gates of reason and thumb its nose at the practical world. If it couldn't, it wouldn't be hope. However, it does operate with its own system of insight, concentrating on goals instead of obstacles.

In religion we talk of a "leap of faith," a religious belief arrived at not by simple logic, but by a complexity of emotions and thoughts. One day your entire universe lights up, and you say, "This is true!" Then, there is the leap that is called falling in love. *She's the one,* you realize. *I love her.* It comes out of nowhere and does not go away.

The leap of hope is very much the same. It is made up of a person's dreams, of memories and passions, tempered by past experiences and upbringing, propelled by a personal view of life and by a deeply ingrained spiritual makeup. Hope is imaginative, but it is no figment of the imagination. It is powerful, it is forward-looking, it is success-oriented. It seeks the best.

Your second fear: *Our hopes did not come true in the past; our fears always did.*

That may be because we easily recall that our worst fears were realized. Rarely do we remember that at another time our wildest hopes also materialized. Maybe your problem lies in the fact that you don't know how to combine the two. Spinoza once said, "No hope is unmingled with fear; no fear unmingled with hope." That is the natural way of things. Every sensible person has a legitimate fear of real danger. If we didn't, we would probably launch the most unattainable ventures. In any new undertaking you have to fear the miscalculations and misjudgments, but you must also visualize the possibilities—and never lose sight of them. The balance between hope and fear is what keeps us in motion. When you appreciate the difference between them, you will understand both better.

The third fear is the hardest to define, but it is an all-important one. It is the fear that, if God is important in fulfilling our hopes, *we may not be able to find Him to help us.* Let me say this right away: When we deal with hope, we *must* deal with God. The energy that propels hope is a spiritual force. Acknowledging this enables you to locate your suffering, which you are hoping to end, on a far larger landscape, and to end the isolation of your pain. It is not so difficult. I am reminded of the words of the theologian Thomas Merton in his masterpiece, *The Seven Storey Mountain*:

> When it comes to accepting God's own authority about things that cannot possibly be known in any other way except as revealed by His authority, people consider it insanity to incline their ears and listen. Things that cannot be known in any other way they cannot accept from this source. And yet they will meekly and passively accept the most appalling lies from newspapers when they scarcely need to crane their necks to see the truth in front of them, over the top of the sheet they are holding in their hands.

Simply incline your ears and listen; as so many of us yearn to. We have a spiritual need so strong that it is a craving, a cry for meaning in a senseless world. Often it is a need that has nothing to do with formal religion. We are reaching out to somehow make a connection, unaware that even as we do that we are speaking to God. We move from there to what Judaism calls *kavanah*—a feeling so profound that it transforms a mere connection into a relationship. When you ask God for something you cannot do without, you do it with *kavanah*.

You might even begin your plea by apologizing for what, to Him, must be trivia.

You might admit that you don't deserve what you want, that in fact there are some things you did that need to be forgiven before you are entitled to *anything* from Him.

When you are doing this, you are saying, "God, You are the one who can change my life. Now help me." This is a profound tribute, and the results can be astonishing.

Say the following every morning, say it every night:

- I know You care and I trust You.
- I will try to be the person You want me to be.
- I will work at growing closer to You.
- I love You. I hope You love me.
- I will return Your kindness.

A spiritual connection with God is not a beeper signal that starts and then stops. It is a bonding, a mystical union you are striving for. When you have achieved it, you will find that, wondrously, it goes two ways—it is a getting that is giving, a giving that is getting. The two actions are actually a part of the same process.

Here is an example. Two old friends of mine were

having a small party for their fiftieth wedding anniversary. Amid the clinking of glasses and the toasts, the wife glanced out the window and noticed an elderly laborer trudging home from work. It was a bleak December evening and she felt that he must be cold and hungry. She ran to the door, opened it, and called to him to come in.

"No thanks," he said. She persisted and he repeated, "No thanks." Then he added, "I don't need charity."

"It is not charity," she said. "It is an invitation. You seem to be a good person and you must be very tired."

Still he refused.

"Please," she implored. "Do it for my sake."

Finally he relented. "All right," he said. "If you insist. I will come in—but only for a short while."

He did, and he seemed to enjoy himself thoroughly.

What really happened in a spiritual sense was that she was giving, but she was receiving as well. And he was receiving, but also giving. This is what happens with God.

Asking for something you want does not of itself forge a deep relationship. All that it does is strike a bargain—something for nothing. We must go deeper and acknowledge our total dependence upon Him. He is there, waiting—to find Him we have only to look.

So, no matter what, *never be afraid to hope*. Fear paralyzes us. It provides no energy, gives us no courage, offers no practical solutions: It locks us into nothingness. But *hopes*, like *dreams, come true*—often against all odds. Maybe we simply don't listen to people when they tell us this. Maybe we think it is like wishing on a star or at a wishing well. Yet I cannot count how many stories of triumph I have heard from the dreamers I know. *Whoever thought I would get this far?* People have said this to me as we sat together in the quiet of my study. Or, *she succeeded beyond her wildest dreams,* they have said of someone else. In my experience as a counselor and a rabbi, an overwhelming number of those I know have accomplished the dreams of their youth. When you dream your dreams, never doubt for a minute that you can make them come true some wonderful day.

Conquering the Fear of Hope

ઢ

Keep this list near you at all times. You might tack it to the bulletin board or tuck it into a corner of your mirror. Take it to heart. Do as it says. It can move you in the right direction:

- I am the hero of my own life story—I will behave like one.
- I won't dwell upon the past; the past is over.
- I will be the one, the only one, in charge of my future.
- I will be patient—nothing happens all at once—but not passive.
- I will trust in a Higher Power to help me along the way.
- And—I will trust in myself.

CHAPTER THREE

Hope Is a Building You May Not Have Entered Yet

To live gloriously, we need hope, not security; the freedom not only to succeed, but to fail and come back. The tragedy of life lies not in failing to reach your goals, but having no hope and thus no goals to reach.

—DR. HENRY VISCARDI
Founder, The National Center
for Disabilities Services

ॐ

53

Before you can appreciate the power of hope, you should at least know what it looks like. *Can I measure it? Can I see it, will I know it? When I look beyond my horizons, will it have a shape that I recognize?*

You will. Just listen. First, think of a house with three stories. You will visit it one story at a time, staying on each level for as long as the climate is right. *How will I know that?* Let me tell you how. Follow me.

INCREMENTAL HOPE: This is the first story of the house. It is the basic unit of hope, so common that you may be unconscious of it, yet sensible and perfectly reasonable. I hope to make *more* money, have *more* leisure time, give *more* to my family. No matter what our wishes may be, incremental hope lets us take one step at a time, each heading toward a single solution. Consider, for example, the process of coping with a troubled marriage. Instead of hoping for a return of the passion that had prompted us to marry, which may be an unrealistic aim now, it may be simpler and wiser to hope in stages—first, to be able to communicate without fighting; second, to be able to understand our partner and to sympathize with him or her; and, finally, to develop the kind of compassionate caring that outlasts romantic love—the kind that lasts for a lifetime.

There is, however, one vital factor about incremental hope: *Make sure you know what you are ultimately hoping for.*

Some years ago I met an enterprising immigrant who had been searching for a way to earn a living in this country since he had arrived here. At last he found it and came to tell me. "I want to open a little post office," he said. When he saw my astonished look, he explained that ever since he had come to the city he had noticed something. The only place that was so busy that a line always extended outside the building was the post office near where he lived.

"So that's the business for me," he said. "Not a big one. Just a little post office." When he saw that I was incredulous he agreed to start even smaller: only the stamp concession!

Impossible though this sounds, who could mock him for a dream like this? At its base it had street-smarts reasoning and vision. When he learned better he dropped the idea. But was it so far-fetched a hope as it then seemed? Not at all—today we know that Mail Boxes Etc and similar businesses are thriving everywhere. His hope instincts really were sound! He knew where he was going—one step at a time.

While such hoping appears to make only minimal progress—one step at a time—it is a long leap ahead of those who don't move forward at all.

The Jewish sages teach this truth by telling the tale of the treadmill. On a treadmill, several donkeys were harnessed to a large wheel, which they spun as they trotted around, thereby generating power. The donkeys wore blinders in order to block them from seeing the wheel. Day after day they kept trotting around and around, but the blinders affixed to the sides of their heads tricked them into thinking that they were going straight. One day someone pulled off the blinders—and the animals went crazy!

Even the dumbest animal cannot saunter purposelessly, going in circles all day, and getting nowhere; there is no progress along a wheel. You probably know people who have been wearing blinders for years, but have you been present when the blinders came off? They may go crazy. This would never happen to those who have high hopes.

HIGH HOPES: This is the second story of our building. Here lie our more distant dreams. People with high hopes want to climb far up the ladder, and yet they are not quite ready for the top. Remember that this kind of progress is what God intended for us. He meant us to go forward and never to move only in circles.

Recently I had a conversation with two camp counselors that perfectly illustrates the difference between incremental and high hopes. "Where do you see yourself a year from now?" I asked them.

They thought for a while, then the first answered, "Assistant head counselor."

The other said, "I want to buy into this camp—it's going to make money!"

The first had considered his next likely move, a logical incremental one. The second wanted to own the whole camp and be the boss who hires the counselors—not a step, a pole vault. His is a high hope.

Hopes can be stretched to accommodate situations as they change. You can hope for better, much better, the best, the very best. Exactly how high your hopes go will depend upon the intensity of your desire, your aggressiveness and imagination, and how afraid of failure you may be. High hopes carry risks, but they also carry wondrous possibilities. When should you entertain them? I use one rule of thumb: If you are wondering if the time has come, it usually means indeed it has. Besides, unless you let your hopes soar, they will never reach where you want to be.

The urge to hope high hopes starts very early. When

I was a child growing up in a New York neighborhood, our mothers did not waste words in giving us advice. Even the briefest of instructions were enough to make the difference. For instance, one mother, sending her son off on the first day of high school, stood in the doorway and shouted after him, "Stay out of trouble!"

Around the corner, another mother, on the same day, with another son beginning his high school career, called out, "Bring home A's!"

Three words made all the difference—and the difference was something called hope. One mother concentrated on the negative goal of not causing any harm; the other looked up and beyond that, and charged her son to strive for high honors.

ECSTATIC HOPE: the third story of our house. This is a dream spot close to the sky, far from anything earthbound. Reason doesn't justify it, imagination can't encompass it, only passion can propel it. To those who need it or want it, it is invaluable, even though it is the most dangerous of all hopes—so strong are the chances that it cannot come true. Logical minds find it bizarre. It is totally unreasonable, they say. But isn't all hope unreasonable?

Ecstatic hoping is what people call "hoping against hope." We do it every day—and sometimes we succeed. Will others consider you crazy? Pay no attention. Who dares assume the authority of God Almighty by deciding on the limits of your hope? Whatever it is, don't let anyone steal it from you. Remember this: Ecstatic hope is the hope that leads to miracles.

For example, the mother of an incurably sick child told me that she was desperately hoping for a scientific breakthrough, a cure, before her son's disease entered its terminal stage. I told her to keep hoping, but also to keep in the back of her mind the realization that the chances of her hope coming true were very slim. If she will accept the unlikelihood of fulfillment, she is entirely justified in hoping for something beyond the realm of reason, transcendental perhaps, but not literally impossible.

The longer the rope, the lower the sag. The more ecstatic the hope, the less likely it is to come true. You must accept this in advance, otherwise you will feel betrayed.

Miracles happen every day and we don't even realize it. You visit a friend in a town in Arizona and inexplicably decide to remain there and build your life in that city. You pick up a book in the library and it opens a new world for you, a world that will define your future. You walk down an ordinary street and see a face in the crowd ahead. You follow the girl with the face—and you have loved that face now for thirty years. Our destinies, our careers, our marriages, often grow out of miracles that we never call by that name—that is, until we look back and say, "What a miracle that was!"

Ecstatic hope is the hope that can reach that very high level. Reason, which has marvelous uses in everyday life, simply cannot fathom what such hope can do. But please, I urge you, don't be such a child of the twentieth century that you listen only to reason and feel that it would be futile to ask for a miracle for yourself.

Miracles are out there waiting for you—just look. Think of those you have heard happening to others: "He was such an idiot in college and now he's the head of a Fortune 500 company." "We thought she was a klutz— and look at the way she can dance!" "The doctor said she could not have children and she is about to have her fourth!"

In medical annals there is what is called *spontaneous remission*, in which a disease, meticulously documented by reputable scientists, goes into remission—tumors shrink, symptoms disappear, pain stops. Why? No one knows. It cannot be explained by medical science.

Perhaps you call these happenings aberrations. But when aberrations happen to you, to your child, to your spouse—well, then they are miracles! Don't let anyone talk you out of hoping for one. Hope for the best; hope for a miracle. Hope works magic on us all. Isn't it true that when you expect a major change in your future, you begin to plan for it, sometimes to act almost as if it had already happened? In your daydreams you move into the future—as if you had already married the man you are engaged to, enrolled in college, taken the new job, moved into the new house, had the baby, achieved recognition.

The fact is, when you decide to hope for a specific goal, you already are halfway there! Magic moments! Miracle of miracles.

We cannot live full lives without a specific goal toward which our energies drive us. That is what hope does. To be productive we need growth. We need to try to do more today than we did yesterday. It is the tension of the bow that propels the arrow. The tauter the string, the more powerful the shot.

Dean Dominick Purpura, of the Albert Einstein College of Medicine in New York, tells his students: "Yes, you are under pressure, but pressure is what makes pearls in oysters."

Of course, there are times when we must have tranquillity, too. Focusing on the future should not mean mortgaging the *entire* present. Today is too short to worry only about tomorrow. Remember, however, that hope gives the present a special meaning. It becomes part of a larger design, not just an end in itself.

A Presbyterian minister told me a story that illustrates this very well. (I have since heard that it is an old story, but I will tell it again.) A bricklayer was asked to help to build the new town church, using his own free time. He agreed.

At seven o'clock one evening, his son came to the site with his dinner. "Dad, aren't you tired of laying bricks all night, after you've done it all day?" he asked. The father answered, "All day I lay bricks; now I am building a church."

The future gives *new meaning* to the present—a glow suffuses the landscape at dawn before the day breaks. And hope for the future *empowers* the present. Think about it. A future project carries its own excitement and enables us to function on a higher level. Say, for example, you decide to build an extra room in your attic for your ten-year-old because you are expecting a new baby in the fall. Normally, who in the world wants to spend a summer at a job like that? But as you work you find yourself smiling; there is an unborn baby in your future. What could you look forward to more than that?

We not only go *up* the stairs of our three-story hope structure, but down them also, as hope remains the loyal servant of our better lives. One of the truly magical qualities of hope is its ability to reinvent itself to adapt to changing conditions.

Take as an example the case of Roberta. When Roberta was twenty she had a clear picture of what her future husband would look like, how much in love with her he would be, what income he would have, what business or profession she would prefer him to have.

Roberta is now thirty and still single. Her hopes have

altered considerably. Looks are not very important anymore. She is doing well in her career, so the size of his income is not so important. There still must be love, but now, Roberta says that even love is not absolute. "After all," she says, "companionship is more fundamental to a good marriage than love—anyway, he'll learn to love me. But he must be considerate and decent." Hope has shrunk from a search for the best and the most to good enough. Hope can do it. And it will—she has learned to rationalize her hopes to the sensible dimensions she now can easily realize.

Six Ways to Beat the Odds

❧

- Do not trust statistics; the ones you see quoted may not apply to you at all.
- Do not waste your energy denying there is a problem—use it instead to find the solution.
- Always leave a door open—in fact, leave as many doors open as you can.
- Study others who have succeeded in doing what you want to do. For now, ignore anyone who failed.
- Hook up with God—His partnership can save your life.
- Never say never.

CHAPTER FOUR

Love and Marriage—
Harbingers of Hope

From the womb of Hope have emerged the twin blessings of Faith and Love to enrich all humankind.

S amuel Johnson once declared that a second marriage is a triumph of hope over experience. He may have been right, but he did not go far enough. *Any* marriage, so long as it works, is a triumph of hope over experience.

Johnson was being cynical about the much-touted ecstasy of love and the legendary difficulties of married life. But his observation provides a sharp insight into the nature of marriage. I believe he is saying that love entices us by holding out the persistent hope for a tomorrow more glorious than today. Every marriage should be endowed with love, but for the marriage to grow, the love must be propelled by enduring hope that will carry it into the future.

Like so many other things in life, marriage is an art that has to be learned. Ideally we set our goals and formulate our hopes from the day of our wedding onward. If you did not do this then, do it now. Keep your hopes high, but do not put them so far beyond your reach that you will grow too discouraged to try. Remember, too, that if there is hope *in* your marriage there is hope *for* your marriage.

Nine Hopes for Your Wedding Day— and for Every Day Thereafter

- I hope that we will always feel about each other the way we feel today.
- I hope that we will create a home that is a cocoon of warmth for us and for our children.
- I hope that money and social standing will never grow more important than love.
- I hope that I'll never try to change my partner.
- I hope that I will be able to hold my temper, even when I know I'm right.
- I hope that I will be reasonable when she is enraged— and that she will be the same.
- I hope that every disagreement we have will end with a new feeling of peace.
- I hope that I won't ever think of marriage only as a substitute for loneliness.
- I hope that we will grow old together.

When you have been married for a time and you argue (and you will), you may be surprised to learn that soon you really may forget what you are arguing about.

I was once the adviser to a medical student and his wife who fought incessantly. So unraveled had their relationship become that they were fast heading toward divorce. We started to do some probing, to find out what they were actually fighting about. They were astonished to find that at the bottom of it was money—or, rather, the lack of it. They were always short of cash. This was wonderful, I told them—a problem that was easily solved. There is an old saying, "A single coin in an empty pot makes a lot of noise."

Wasn't it reasonable, I asked them, that the time would come when they had a full pot? Of course it was. After they finished their studies and paid their college loans, that problem would no longer exist. All they had to do to enjoy today was to live it while knowing what lay in the future. It is like borrowing from a marriage equity fund, I told them. You borrow for your marriage of tomorrow, based on the collateral value of your living together today. All they had to do now was live on a very reasonable hope.

Problems more complex and long-standing than theirs have solutions, too, if you will look for them. But just as couples so often don't know *why* they fight, they don't know *how* to stop. They don't know how to look for the answers they need; it is something else they have to learn. Follow the rules below and a new married world may open to you.

Hope Is Love's Oxygen

Denis de Rougemont, an expert on the history of love in the Western world, says that society appears hell-bent on its most insane experiment—basing marriage, which is supposedly permanent, on romance, which is short-lived.

Married love needs depth, and a resonance, that comes from hope. Marriage needs to go somewhere or it will die of monotony and predictability.

Postponing a clear picture of the future of your marriage until you reach some turning point, a corner in your life—a new job, another degree—is to create a hopeless union. With a hope orientation, a marriage can look forward to more assured success. When you stand at the threshold of a marriage and don't envision great plans for the future, you invite drift before you embark.

Marriage Founders When It Drifts

I have found that when a couple hopes together they have a better chance of staying together. Hope counteracts drift by always turning the marriage toward the very next event. You always experience an unfolding of new possibilities on the horizon. "What's next on the agenda?" is a good thing to ask after you feel a special sense of achievement. Or try, "Where do we *grow* from here?" Success breeds success. This is the hope orientation for marriage. Wives and husbands should pose these questions to one another at every turn in the family's history. This does not deny the wonders of the present, but opens exciting vistas to the wonders of yet another good future.

Marriage also founders when it crashes into perennial arguments, as the boulders jut out from below the surface of your relationship. Yes, even quarreling, that staple of every marriage, requires a hope that says: "Hold it, there is a tomorrow." If there is no faith in a tomorrow for the marriage, what will enable you to transcend the daily frictions of the present? I see this time and again; what causes a marriage to finally disintegrate is not difference of opinion, but an *in*difference of opinion—a sense of hopelessness. When husbands and wives get to a point of just biding time, just living from day to day, the marriage is in trouble. But if at least one of you sees a future, there is hope.

Four Musts for Launching a Hopeful Marriage

- Begin by deciding with your spouse that your marriage is worth the hope for a better future. Then, analyze why this hope is worthwhile. For example, maybe it's worthwhile because you experience at least some wonderful moments together—on vacation, at a party, at a child's graduation or other celebration.

- Articulate, consciously and purposefully, some of the hopes of your marriage. Start with the hope that you can navigate those sharp boulders that squat stubbornly in peaceful waters and block a lifetime of wholesome relationships.

  Your hope may look far off, but one partner at least needs to sight it in the future. Do this exercise of intentional hoping. Leap out of the present, temporarily, and fly into the future. List all the possibilities of hope—for both of you as individuals, for both of you as part of a family, for the children, for the jobs you now have, for the place you would most like to live in.

- Jump-start the ship of love for deeper waters, by examining the depths of your relationship, and what you feel deeply about. Avoid entering the shallows and crashing again.

- Watch it! If your marriage does not include hope, you are both living below your psychic means.

Six Rules for Making Your Marriage Last Forever

ॐ

- Decide that yours is a marriage worth saving.
- Force yourself to communicate with your spouse about what the future holds. Forget the jagged rocks in the waters of your marriage now—make up your mind to reach the smooth seas that lie beyond them.
- Let the partner who is best at charting the future (and, very often, one is better than the other) lead the way.
- Under that leadership, do this exercise together. Project yourselves into tomorrow, listing all your hopes—as individuals, as a family, for your children, for the jobs you have now, for the ones you would like, for the places where you most want to live.
- Having thus decided what you want, don't be afraid to go after it. Remember, only in the shallows is your boat about to crash.
- Leave your milestones in your past. Don't expect memories to help you. It is tempting to try to recapture the lost excitement of falling in love, to call back the magic of certain happy times. Don't do it. Ask instead, *what's next*—where are we going *now*?

CHAPTER FIVE

Sweet Are the Uses of Adversity

Power based on others is undependable. Hope is power based on yourself—and it gives you the energy and strength to fight back when adversity strikes.

ใช

W e may be the poorer for it, but it is hard for us, in our contemporary world, to feel secure about anything we are asked to accept without positive proof. This is why hope still puzzles us. There is no proof positive that hope will certifiably raise us out of despair.

A famous teacher of mysticism recently tried illustrating hope's spiritual power with a symbol. Take the letter *M*, he said, as in the word *Me*. It is a selfish letter, its two legs facing downward, rooted in the barter of material life, representing only the self. Then take the letter *W*, as in *We*. Its two sides face upward as if reaching to Heaven, indicating a spiritual sharing with others. Be guided in life by *W* and not by *M*.

Maybe a symbol will help you and maybe it will not. I can only urge you to believe in the power of hope because it is a positive, clear, critical, necessary part of the human apparatus. Not only does it enable us to survive bad times, it helps turn them around. Not only does it make life bearable, it makes it a game we are eager to play once again—and win.

Novelist Elizabeth Berg wrote a moving book, *Talk Before Sleep*, about the death of her closest friend from breast cancer at the age of forty-three. In one passage she writes:

> No matter how frightened and discouraged I become about the future, I look forward to it. In spite of everything I see all around me every day, in spite of all the times I cry when I read the newspaper, I have a shaky assurance that everything will turn out fine. I don't think I'm the only one. Why else would the phrase "Everything's all right" ease a deep and troubled place in so many of us? We just don't know, we never know so *much*, yet we have such faith. We hold our hand over our hurts and lean forward full of yearning and forgiveness. It is how we keep on, this kind of hope.

The writer Truman Capote was a mercurial personality, but to those who knew him well he offered the gift of friendship—and the gift of friendship so often goes hand in hand with the gift of hope. He wrote the following to his first editor, Mary Louise Aswell, during a difficult time in her life:

> All human life has its seasons, and no one's personal chaos can be permanent; winter after all does not last

forever, does it? There is summer, too, and spring, and though sometimes when branches stay dark and the earth cracks with ice, one thinks they will never come, that spring, that summer, but they do, and always.

Recently, Yoko Ono, widow of the Beatle John Lennon, was asked if, in retrospect, she could account for the incredible phenomenon the Beatles were in their day. She gazed out over Strawberry Fields in Central Park, a memorial to their music. "I think they had so much hope," she said. "We all had such hope then. And when you have that kind of hope you can accomplish anything."

The easiest way to explain how hope bonds our lives may be to begin not at the beginning, but at the end. It is such a strong emotion that even hopes that *don't* come true have a powerful effect upon us. Shakespeare may have said it best: "Sweet are the uses of adversity, / Which, like the toad, ugly and venomous, / Wears yet a precious jewel in his head."

When I was a youngster I memorized a poem by Robert Browning Hamilton:

> I walked a mile with Pleasure
> She chatted all the way,
> But left me none the wiser
> For all she had to say.

I walked a mile with Sorrow,
And ne'er a word said she;
But, oh the things I learned from her
When Sorrow walked with me.

I was a young rabbi when a colleague called me with an urgent request. His fifteen-year-old son was lethargic and uninterested in virtually everything. In school his grades were hovering at the bottom. He asked me to go with him to see Dr. G., a family friend who was also a school psychologist.

It is long ago now, but I still remember Dr. G.'s exact words: "He's close to the bottom? Let him fall!" I could not believe what I was hearing. "The shock of hitting bottom," he said, "will hurt him, and it may rouse him. If it does, you will have no more worries. If it doesn't, we'll have to scrape him off the floor and work on him to get him up gradually."

When he heard this pronouncement, my friend scowled and turned to me. "Would *you* do this to your son?" he asked me.

I recommend it, I said. And when his son did hit bottom, the shock resulted in his only hope being "up." Today, that lethargic teenager is a professor of mathematics at an Ivy League University, and hardly speaks to us lesser intellectuals.

One reason Alcoholics Anonymous is so successful is

because it is based on the simple proposition that an alcoholic cannot help himself until he is in total despair and has lost all his illusions, all his hopes. Only then can he see clearly that, left to his own devices, he is beyond healing. When we hit bottom and reach ultimate despair, we have no choice but to embrace the truth, look up, and start to climb out of the pit.

Jean-Paul Sartre, the existentialist philosopher, once said, "Human life begins on the far side of despair." It can—and very often does.

Five Uses of Adversity That Really Work

ॐ

It may be difficult to believe that we can learn from adversity, yet it is our best teacher. Think what it can do for us if we let it.

- *It can open our eyes.* It can force us to look at our life and our lifestyle, to let go of old, inappropriate hopes, fruitless love affairs, dependencies which hold us back, self-deception which feeds our ego but does nothing else.
- *It can make us grow in ways we never knew.* Storms demand more alertness from us than sunshine does. From somewhere deep inside we can find more patience, more endurance, more courage, more concentration. Then, when we are sure there are no resources left, we find even more. Try it.
- *It can give us the precious gift of compassion.* Nobody helps the homeless as much as those who have known homelessness; nobody knows pain so well as someone who has suffered. Defeat gives us the rare gift of empathy.
- *It can teach us a universal truth: Life is not fair.* People die before they should; lovers who belong together quarrel and part; a conglomerate seizes a company and

we lose our job; someone else gets the lead in the school play. When we are very young we believe that life will be trouble-free and justice always will triumph—the quicker we learn that isn't so, the easier time we will have.

- *If we are very thoughtful it can lead us to God.* Good fortune rarely does that. It is human nature to feel when we lose anything that someone else had a hand in our misfortune. We may blame a Higher Power—when we do that we are at the same time acknowledging Him! A strange spiritual dynamic gets set in motion: After blaming God, we can begin appealing to Him for help out of adversity—and with that we have found the road to our future.

CHAPTER SIX

Stories of Hope

Look at the barriers you encounter only as navigation problems. They are not dead ends, but merely detours on the road to where you want to go.

In many years of counseling, not to mention years of living, I have not ceased to be surprised at the resiliency of the human heart. I have witnessed great sorrow and fear and pain; yet I know there is no lasting defeat in life. I know this because when I have least expected to see it, I have always witnessed hope. These are a few of the stories I remember best, of times when hope becomes a shining beacon.

Once, I thought that education and enlightenment would end prejudice. Now I know that such a hope is foolish. It is more realistic to hope *not* that it will disappear, but that we will be able to control it.

I learned from a single incident as a military chaplain that there is indeed much to hope for in regard to religious and racial prejudice—but *not* that it will eventually disappear. Now I hope that good people everywhere will realize that we must confront it and fight it at every turn, and that only in that way will we keep it at bay.

I was a young chaplain in Fort Benning, Georgia, during the Korean War and I wanted to be the one to make a difference. When Brotherhood Week came, I proposed turning it into a meaningful program by featuring chaplains of different faiths who would answer the same questions, basing their answers on the tenets of their own religion. We developed a script that we agreed upon, and we rehearsed beforehand in order to avoid surprises. In addition to me, there was a Southern Baptist minister, a Congregationalist minister, and a Jesuit priest. The command chaplain, Monsignor John Kelly, served as moderator. We aired on Georgia television on a Sunday in February.

Everything went as planned until the final question: "In your religion will these other chaplains receive eternal reward?" Both the Congregationalist and I answered that *all* good people would achieve their reward in Heaven, no matter their faith. The Jesuit reasoned that there was a baptism of desire for otherwise good people who weren't taught the truth—so that I, for example, could get to Heaven.

Then a chaplain who was a Southern Baptist turned to me and said without flinching, "Rabbi, I believe you are going to Hell!" I was caught badly off guard. Instinctively I shot back, "But I am not yet prepared to leave your native state of Georgia." The monsignor quickly ended the program.

I was enraged. My instinct was to punch him or shake him or at least to tell *him* to go to hell. I ran from the studio, went to my quarters, put on civvies, and drove my old Chevy toward Columbus.

As I drove I could feel my blood pressure rising. Why would this man want to hurt me this way? Why would he rehearse one answer, then give another? On the other hand, how could I be so naive? I gave the man a platform. I did not even know whether, as a junior officer, I should have reacted to a major as I did, even though he had humiliated my religion. My head couldn't contain the ideas colliding inside it. Maybe, I thought, I was not cut out for such combat.

I was so upset that I wasn't safe at any speed. A police car suddenly materialized in my rearview mirror and flagged me down. I gave the officer my driver's license. He took it and went back to his car to write his ticket, but returned almost at once without it. "Sorry, Chaplain, but do be more careful next time," he said. I was puzzled. How could he have known I was a chaplain? Then I looked closely at my license and for the first time noticed a faint blue cross superimposed on its face, something undoubtedly used for all chaplains.

Something was troubling me about both these events. I drove onto the shoulder of the road, leaned my head back, and tried to think clearly. A message was breaking through. God was tapping my brain.

Then it dawned on me. That chaplain saw me as outside the bounds of Christianity and, despite the fact that

I had done no wrong, he consigned me to Hell. The cross on my license placed me within the realm of Christian religions and, despite the fact that I violated the law, it protected me. Protecting me was as wrong as damning me. Thank you, but no thank you—I want neither the sting nor the honey.

I turned my car around, drove back to Fort Benning, and had them reissue me an unmarked license. Then I rushed back to my office. There I found a message from the command chaplain ordering me to attend a staff meeting at 0900 at chaplain headquarters.

As I stepped into the room at headquarters the following morning, I saw that it was filled with all twenty-seven chaplains on the post. The monsignor began, "I call this meeting to make a public reprimand, because of an infraction that was made publicly. Chaplain, you violated the trust the United States Army placed in you to promote brotherhood. You spoke words of hatred instead of words of Christian charity. You will depart your office at Main Post Chapel, and hereafter be assigned to Sand Hill Chapel at the northern perimeter. I will place this reprimand in your 201 file, and it will remain with you to the end of your career."

No one moved. It was so quiet you could hear jaws drop.

The chaplain asked to speak. He was a stocky, broad-shouldered man, and he rose to his full military bearing and looked the monsignor straight in the eye and said, "I know what's ticking you off, sir. But I believed, and I still do believe, that as a man of God I have an obligation to tell the truth, even if I had to deviate from that script, sir."

There was a heavy silence. I would have counseled any rabbi in my position at that moment to keep his composure—and also his seat. I didn't. I felt all eyes upon me.

"Chaplain, sir," I said, "I truly do not mind your telling me that I am going to Hell. That's what you believe, and you have a right to that belief. We are all in uniform to protect that right. But I have a question for you: Were you *informing* me that I am going to Hell, or were you *accusing* me of it? You see, if you wanted to inform me, you could have sat me down in your office and told me the news. But when you turn on me in a public forum to proclaim it, you are accusing me, and you are also condemning the Jewish people. That, sir, is inflammatory."

The chaplain jumped to his feet. "I will say what I believe, in any way that I like, and you will not chide me. This is a Christian country, and Georgia is a Christian state, and I am a Christian minister. I can tell any Jew that he will go to Hell, anytime. That is what I believe, and that is gospel truth." The chaplains shouted him down, and the monsignor ordered him to sit down.

I was in control, but I asked to speak again. "Chaplain, sir, do you know when the Jewish people suffered the worst pogroms in history? At Easter time. Do you know why? Because pastors preached that the Jews killed Jesus, which as you know is not true. Now, I do believe, sir, that you would not want to trigger a pogrom. But that is what has always happened after public pronouncements such as yours. You might think it can't happen in the United States—and I assure you that it won't happen, because good people will fight it with their lives—but don't you think it would arouse terrible hatred? I have nothing more to say, except to repeat that the Jewish people do believe if you, sir, act decently, you will go to Heaven."

What I learned from that chaplain colored my entire career. I learned that I never will allow my dignity to cave in before bullies or bigots. I learned to stand tall, no matter who stands over me. And mostly I learned never to lose hope in the brotherhood of mankind.

And I will not go to Hell.

SHARON

Sharon Blass is a bright young woman, sophisticated in her interests, successful in her career. She first came to my office for counseling because she had an explosive split with her parents. The reason: She had insisted upon aborting her first pregnancy.

Her mother and father were survivors of the Holocaust, so the deliberate breaking of the chain of generations was totally beyond the pale to them. Sharon said, however, that she was not ready for a child at this stage in her life. She had a new marriage, a new job, and new friendships she was absorbed in cultivating.

Eventually she might want to have a child, but not now. Horrified, her parents left her apartment without another word. I tried to explain to Sharon that, having so narrowly escaped death themselves, it was natural for them to feel that they were miraculously privileged and must pass along their good fortune to the generations that would follow.

It was futile. Sharon had no feelings about the future of her family or about her religion. "I'm sorry," she said. "My parents will just have to work that out for themselves."

Two years later she sought me out again. This was a pale, trembling shadow of the young woman I had seen before. She had not spoken to her parents since our last meeting, but she had changed; she was ready to have a child.

The problem was that now she could not get pregnant. Two reliable fertility clinics in New York found no biological or physiological cause preventing conception, but it was not happening. Now Sharon wanted a child more than anything else in life.

After several painful weeks of counseling, Sharon told me that something was on her mind—she would like to reopen her relationship with God. "Maybe I was too brazen about religion," she said. "Now I wish I could talk to Him."

"What about?" I asked.

"Well," she said, "first I admit I want to scream at Him for letting the Holocaust happen and causing me to lose so many members of my family. Then I want to ask about my baby. But, Rabbi, I can't do this alone. I have no connection to God. I feel like a hypocrite. Will you connect me, please?"

I smiled at her. "But you are connected already," I said. "Haven't you been hoping intensely for a child? Who do you think you were addressing? Who do you think could make those hopes come true?"

I will never forget her exclamation: "This is crazy. I really have been hoping to God—and I'm not sure I even *believe* in Him!"

"Remember," I said, "God has a history of performing miracles. Now you must ask Him for one—and enlist your mother and father in hoping, too."

"Yes, of course," she said. "At least I'll have my parents back. That means a lot to me."

First Sharon adopted a Vietnamese baby and named

her Tikvah, which is Hebrew for hope. Just a year after the adoption, she gave birth to a son—to a grandson!

When Sharon began to hope for a baby, she was unconsciously acknowledging that God had the power to help her. She opened a door and began a bonding with a power higher than she. And her hopes came true.

STANDING TALL

One thing about hope doesn't change: You will find it by looking upward. It has not been spotted in the gutter yet.

I was waiting for a bus in front of Bishop Hill School in Riverdale, when I noticed a crowd of youngsters cheering on two boys who were fighting. Eventually, the short scrappy kid flattened the tall skinny one, who tripped off the curb and into the street. I broke it up, and asked the scrappy kid why he was fighting.

"It's none of your business," he said.

"Are you afraid to tell me?" I said.

He assured me he was afraid of no one, absolutely no one.

"So you simply won't tell me?"

"Okay, I will tell you. The beanpole always calls me little squirt and peewee. So I showed him. Now look who's bigger!" He bellowed to the tall kid, who was struggling. "Hey, little runt!" Everyone laughed.

"I understand you," I said. "I had the same trouble when I was young. People always called me shrimp, pee-wee, peanut, junior."

"Oh yeah?" He was clearly surprised that someone of my advanced years could ever understand. "What'd you do?"

"Well, at first I used to fight back, too. If you must know, I really got the hell knocked out of me—they were all bigger than I was. One day I knocked a big kid down, just as you did now. At that moment my uncle came walking by and he broke up the fight. Then he pulled over a chair and told me to stand on it."

Out of the corner of my eye I saw a bench at the bus stop a few feet away. "I'll show you. Come here!" I lured the two young fighters over to the bench. I told the tall kid to stand next to the bench, and the short one to stand on top of the bench.

"Now," I said to the little one, "tell me who is bigger?" He grinned. "Me again!" And he raised one hand in triumph, like a prizefighter after the count. The other kids watched and hooted.

"That's what I said to my uncle. Then my uncle said to me, 'You klutz! Instead of knocking him down, you climb higher!' From then on I knew that I couldn't spend the next hundred years fighting everybody who called me 'little.' So I started climbing—and I've been climbing ever since."

I could not resist adding one thing. "Hey, kid," I said, "are you a Catholic?"

"Sure. What's it to you?"

"I'll tell you another secret. When you stand higher, you're closer to God."

"Thanks, Padre."

Focus your hope on your own achievements. You will rise.

MARLA

At two in the morning the doorbell rang. Standing in the doorway, soaked from the pouring rain, was a student, twenty-seven-year-old Marla, wild-eyed and at the edge of hysteria. She shoved her six-week-old daughter into my arms and screamed, "Take her; I might kill her!" Then she vanished into the night.

I called to her once, twice; but she ran. I was in my bathrobe and couldn't chase after her. My wife Shirley was startled. We had not cared for an infant in years. "What kind of mother is she?" Shirley said. "What could be wrong with her? Call the police! She might kill herself."

I didn't believe she would commit suicide, and I managed to calm Shirley. We settled on praying that Marla would do nothing drastic. I called her house five times over the course of the night and reached only her answering machine. The baby awakened every hour crying. At last I found an all-night market that sold baby formula. At dawn, my wife was preparing the formula and cooing at the baby.

At six o'clock in the morning, no Marla; at six-thirty, no Marla; at seven, nothing. When I called there was still only her voice on the machine—its cheerfulness seemed to mock us. I began to worry. Maybe Shirley was right; maybe I should have called the police.

At ten after seven the doorbell rang. Marla! "I'm sorry," she said. "How is my baby? Give her to me."

"How is your baby? We have been worried sick! How are you?"

"I'm fine. Please. Just give me my baby."

"Of course we will give you your baby. But not yet. First we have to find out what is wrong."

She said, "I'm better. Please. I'm better."

I said, "How can you be better? Did you solve your problem in five hours? I cannot let you leave here until I know that you can work things out. Now sit down, let's have breakfast, and let's talk."

She came into the house, we put the baby in our grandchildren's Portacrib, and Shirley made coffee. We needed Valium, not caffeine, but we settled.

Marla began to sob quite pitifully.

"I'm not a bad mother," she moaned. "I'm a good mother."

"Of course, you are," I said. "I know that."

"You must understand. Melissa was crying, and I thought I was literally going to choke her. I was scared to death. Do you understand that?"

"The truth, Marla, is no. I really don't. How could you kill your baby? Don't you love her? Parents get overwrought. But killing? You wouldn't."

She wiped her eyes. "You don't understand. I know myself."

"Then why don't you trust yourself?" Those words tripped the wire, and she exploded into hysteria. She began to shake uncontrollably.

"That's exactly the point," she screamed. "Exactly. I can't trust myself anymore. Oh, God, I can't trust myself!"

I pleaded with her to tell me the story. "You know my mother," she said. "Nice lady, right? I'm sorry to hurt her. Really. I love her. But I have to tell somebody. She's crippled me." Marla then began a story that made us weep with her. Until she was fifteen she was regularly abused by her mother—a broken arm, scorched fingers, an earlobe pulled until it tore, epithets, threats. The worst memory of all was of the night her mother tried to choke her—almost to death. Marla's hand reached for her neck. She lifted up her scarf, the trademark she always wore, and showed us where her mother had dug her nails into her. There were no marks anymore. No matter, Marla still wears scarves.

"Rabbi," she whispered, "this is the greatest fear of my life—I am my mother's daughter; I inherited her genes."

My heart sank. Marla was convinced that her past had a stranglehold on her future, that there was no hope for her. I learned then the ultimate abuse is when the abused believes that she must become an abuser.

"It's going to be all right, Marla. Between us, we will work it out."

We saw that Marla needed our care and we put her in one of our vacant bedrooms, where she feel asleep.

I then called a friend of mine, an excellent and sympathetic psychotherapist. He canceled two appointments to come to our house, and planned on intensive therapy to root out Marla's past, so that she could revisit her childhood experiences through adult eyes.

At the same time, I was going to try to stimulate her self-worth so that she could regain her personal strength and her faith in herself. This seemed like a tall order— but I couldn't simply sit down and chat about her lack of self-confidence. I decided upon an unusual approach.

I told the psychotherapist that I would study with Marla for five sessions. He raised his professional eyebrows, and stuck his tongue in his cheek. "Study? Really?"

"Really," I said.

With Marla, I was going to investigate role models to replace the only model she knew, her mother. There would be famous women from long ago who, having found themselves in worse situations than Marla's—surrounded by worse role models, raised in more dysfunctional families—were self-willed, forceful, in-control women who had masterfully overcome their environment. The women were the heroines of Genesis—Sarah, Rebekah, and Rachel!

I would then make the setting more familiar, and focus on modern paragons, such as Eleanor Roosevelt and Israel's Golda Meir—about whom then Prime Minister David Ben-Gurion once said: "She's the best man in my cabinet!" Through these studies Marla could learn values she never learned at home—honor, strength, self-love, self-worth.

One day, five weeks later, Marla made a breakthrough. She announced to me, "Rabbi, I made a discovery—I have an extended family." "Really," I said. "I thought you had no siblings."

She smiled for the first time in all these weeks. "I found out that my mother is only one woman in a long line of mothers. They start with those tough ladies in Genesis. They're *my* mothers too!"

"Who's to say I didn't inherit from them? Rabbi, I did. And I'm telling you, I can make it. I know I can make it. I'm sure of it."

I was dumbfounded. It was actually working. Never in my life had psychotherapy and the Bible worked in tandem. I said: "Marla. Go home and get yourself a life!"

She thanked me and left. Then she opened the door and stuck her head in: "Rabbi, for the first time I have hope. You'll see. I'm gonna make it." Then she closed the door and opened it again and said, with more than a touch of whimsy, "Rabbi, I love you."

THE SHEPHERD

One night several years ago, while visiting Jerusalem, I was stricken with the sharpest pain I had ever experienced. I was rushed to the hospital where, suddenly, inexplicably, the pain disappeared and did not return. For two weeks thereafter, however, I was kept under observation. This is how I met Jacob, the shepherd.

He was one of my roommates, and I was glad for his company and a new experience. I had never seen a sheep until I was eighteen, much less met a shepherd—and I'm sure that in the entire Lamm patrimony not one was a leader of lambs. Jacob was in his forties, leather-skinned, laconic, strong—and very serious. I asked him how he kept his mind occupied during long stretches of isolation and inactivity. He read philosophy, he said: Plato's *Republic*, Aristotle's *Rhetoric*, and the medieval Arabic philosophers Averroës and Avicenna. He was a religious skeptic, however, and had read no religious literature, except for the Bible, which he studied only to learn the geography of the Holy Land and the history of the Jewish people. His outlook on life and the world was endlessly fascinating.

At three o'clock one morning I was jarred from sleep by a roomful of doctors and nurses surrounding Jacob's bed. My heart sank. They rushed him to emergency surgery.

Fifteen minutes later, a nurse hurried into the room to tell me that Jacob refused to go into surgery until I had been given this message: "I need a shepherd."

I was completely baffled. I told the nurse that he probably wanted to call one of his shepherd friends. I told her to ask him to tell her more.

She left and returned, reporting that he said, "For a rabbi, you are not very smart." Well, he was right—I didn't have a clue.

I had to think fast. My other roommate, an unlettered boor, said that Jacob was probably delirious. Maybe so. Maybe so.

Then it came to me! Yes! I opened the drawer of his nightstand and pulled out the miniature Book of Psalms, which the Israeli Army gives to new conscripts. I opened the book and said to the nurse, "Tell him I understand. Read Psalm Twenty-three on page forty-two to him: 'The Lord is my shepherd.' Then tell him I will pray to God for him." She ran out and delivered the message. I prayed for him in my room, at his empty bed. Later, she returned to say that he smiled, closed his eyes, and was wheeled into surgery. She thanked me, and left.

At seven o'clock the next morning, an intern came to tell me that Jacob had come through the operation successfully, and was waiting for me in recovery. I rushed to him.

He said to me: "You know that I am a shepherd. Now, you know, dear rabbi, that *even a shepherd needs a shepherd*. I need a shepherd myself, like I am to my little lambs. When my sheep have me, they need nothing. The sheep trust in me. Listen, they don't know where I will go, what I will do. They know only that I am good for them. I think they even love me!

"The truth is that I already met our Great Shepherd, face-to-face—He was just walking with me in the valley of the shadow of death! And I was not afraid!"

He closed his eyes and fell asleep. I kissed his hand and said: "Shalom." Many times later when I was in trouble, I have whispered to myself, "Even a shepherd needs a shepherd." Hope for survival is not always something we can do alone.

MR. B

Dr. Elisabeth Kübler-Ross, who has spent a lifetime motivating terminally ill patients to accept the fact of their impending death, says that even the most accepting of them retains a sense of hope in the midst of their very tangible fears. "It is this," she writes, "which maintains them through days, weeks or months of suffering . . . it remains a form of temporary but needed denial. It encourages them to accept medicines and treatments until the very end."

One of the most impressive examples of this kind of hope I learned from a famed cardiologist, Dr. Bernard Lown, professor of cardiology at Harvard University School of Public Health, who was one of Norman Cousins's physicians and who wrote the introduction to one of Cousins's books. Dr. Lown cited a case that occurred early in his career. Mr. B had had a massive heart attack and his cardiac muscle function was irreparably damaged. His lungs were congested. His heart rate was uncontrollably rapid, the rhythm utterly chaotic.

The physicians had exhausted all their strategies. One morning during his rounds, Dr. Lown was standing with his students at Mr. B's bedside. The patient wore an oxygen mask and seemed oblivious to everything. Dr. Lown commented dryly that Mr. B had a wholesome, very loud, third-sound gallop. This is a very poor sign denoting that the heart muscle is straining and usually failing. The doctors left the moribund patient.

But Mr. B began to recover. Words like "irreparable," "incurable," and "terminal" disappeared from his charts. He improved gradually, until one day Dr. Lown was able to release him from the hospital and he was wheeled, upright and smiling, through the exit door.

Dr. Lown remained utterly perplexed—it could not have been medication that kept this man alive. Months later, Mr. B told him what had happened. He knew the exact moment when his recovery started.

"I was sure the end was near and that you and your staff had given up hope. Then I heard you tell your colleagues that I had a 'wholesome gallop,' so I figured that I still had a lot of kick to my heart and I could not be dying. For the first time my spirits lifted, and I knew that I would recover."

Evidently even hope that comes by mistake can heal, if we give it a chance and believe in it. Physicians and caregivers agree that it is possible for the mind to transform life. Hope is a positive power that gives people an incentive to live and an ability to survive, and it is to be ignored only at the greatest risk.

AKIRA

The Kawakami family moved from Kobe, Japan, to the Bronx, New York, in the seventies, to start a new life and to raise their only child, Akira, to be an American. Four years later, Akira was the valedictorian of his high school class, with a scholarship to Yale. Every day on the way to my office, as I bought a single persimmon from the Kawakamis' fruit stand, they reported on how well he was doing.

One warm night in September, lounging on the steps in front of his house, Akira was gunned down in a blaze of M-16 fire from a passing car, and he lay severely wounded in a pool of blood. Police could not find the shooter, nor any motive.

The Kawakamis were inconsolable. They took turns keeping vigil outside Akira's hospital room, while tending the fruit stand, without which they could not survive. On the second day, Akira's mother crouched in a corner of the hospital room, curled in a ball, rocking back and forth. Akira's father was devastated. He could not reach his wife, he could not reach his son, he could not even leave the hospital to work at the fruit stand.

I visited in the afternoons to try to coax Mrs. Kawakami out of her cocoon. On the fourth day she looked at me with sad eyes. I stretched out my hand and somehow was able to raise her from the floor, and I walked with her silently into the street. The air carried a hint of autumn and the streets were busy, but neither nature nor society paid any attention to what was happening inside the hospital. The outdoors distracted her for a few minutes, but then she wanted to go back inside.

We walked along the winding hospital corridor, scanning the paintings on the walls. She stopped to look at a hand-woven Oriental tapestry of the sun setting on Mount Fuji. What was she seeing? Did the Japanese scene remind her that she should have not left home? Did she and her husband precipitate their son's crisis?

After several minutes, I walked up to the tapestry and turned it around to face the wall. "Why did you do that?" Mrs. Kawakami asked. I said, "I want to explain something to you. I think I can do it if you will look at this tapestry from the opposite side.

"Notice that all you can see is a clutter of threads. Strings shoot off in every direction—knots here, knots there, loose threads everywhere. There's no pattern, it makes no sense. But think of this: When you know there is a masterpiece on the other side you begin to sense meaning and beauty, and you begin to see some plan in this crazy snarl of threads.

"This is how I look at the terrible senseless crime that wounded Akira. When something like this happens, we only see the wild mess of threads, the colors flying in every direction. There appears to be no order, only chaos; no pattern, only a maze. Mrs. Kawakami, if you will think of it, you will see that we spend our whole lives looking at the reverse side, trying to figure out the sense of this world. What does it mean? But, perhaps if you can sense that there is another side, an awesome tapestry of the world that only a Higher Power can see, the wildness may begin to make some sense."

We began to walk away. After a few feet Mrs. Kawakami stopped and turned around to stare at the reversed tapestry. Then she went to see her son.

There is hope for Akira. Medical miracles happen. But prayer also heals in strange and surprising ways. Is there hope for the Kawakamis if Akira does not survive? Yes. Sometimes parents do have to witness their child's death—the most tragic of bereavements—and against all the odds they can survive and live with that haunting memory. In such circumstances hope can direct us to the pattern on the other side, hidden from our eyes.

It has a mysterious quality, this thing called hope, and it works differently in different circumstances to enable us to survive our deepest sorrows.

CARLOS

I learned something recently that I should have known all along—the true agony of the inner city is in the ghetto of the mind, not the ghetto of the streets. More than economic deprivation, it is a lack of hope that is responsible for violence in the ghetto.

The 1992 Los Angeles riots were perpetrated by people choking from a lack of hope. It was a Friday, the day after the riots had begun. I was in my car at the corner of Wilshire Boulevard waiting for the light to change, a mile from the center of the riot area, when I saw a Latino boy of about sixteen, running, falling, getting up again, and dragging himself along the street. Instinctively, I waved him toward my car and opened the door. He crumpled into the front seat. If I had thought about it, I might not have done this—fear makes us all hesitate. He told me his name was Carlos Ramirez, and this was his story:

The tenement building he lived in with his family was set afire and the tenants frantically ran to safety. Carlos found himself surrounded by flames in his room on the sixth floor and couldn't escape. Smoke had forced its way through holes in the walls and the ceiling and he was coughing uncontrollably. Remembering that one should get as close to the ground as possible in a fire, he crawled along the floor toward the front door. The door handle melted and scorched his hand.

He could barely breathe. As he began dragging himself toward the window, he felt something under him. It was the limp body of his sister, dead from asphyxiation. She was the one person in all the world whom he truly loved. He kissed her and sobbed, but realizing he couldn't risk using what little air was left, he crawled along until finally he reached a window. It was locked. As he was telling me this, he kept repeating "my sister, my little sister," and tears streamed down his cheeks.

In the burning room he was thinking clearly and logically. He was, he said, more angry than scared. He was angry at his sister's dying for no reason, angry because he was losing his life for nothing, angry for wasting sixteen years of his sixteen-year life.

"Dammit," he cried out, "I'm busting out of here. I am going to live. I'm going to make it out of here and I'm going to make something of myself. Dammit, I'm going to live!"

I was out of breath just listening to him.

He spotted his father's hammer on the floor of the bedroom and flung it at the window. The glass shattered, the cool air rushed in, and he crawled through the opening onto the ledge. A net was spread below and he leaped. His shoulder and face were slashed from the glass and an arm may have been broken, but he was safe.

He could not contain his rage and, refusing all offers of help, he turned and ran. No one followed him and no one asked where he was running. He ran for blocks until he fell in exhaustion into my car.

Carlos Ramirez was seriously hurt, but his resolve was strengthened. I must have muttered aloud what I was thinking to myself—that he wasn't suffocating from a shortage of oxygen but from a desperate shortage of hope. He heard me and said that he remembered actually thinking something like that during the frantic moments in his apartment.

He had broken through the glass and fled the neighborhood, and now he was angry enough to take on the world. He would mourn his sister, but he was going to try to make himself a future. He asked me to drop him at a Catholic church, where he could catch his breath, think things through, pray a little, and talk to a priest about his future. He opened the car door and walked into his new world.

I was never able to find out how Carlos made out. But I do know there hides inside us all an irrepressible Carlos, striving for a breath of hope that is as important to us as our need for oxygen. Wouldn't it be impossible to live without it? Isn't it hope that propels us forward to realize our own destiny?

Now you and I know that this young man's passion is not a solution to all the problems of the ghetto. It was a solution, however, for one person. This sixteen-year-old gave me courage and a renewed conviction about the future of America's children, including those for whom we often give up hope. I expect to read someday about Carlos's return to this neighborhood, which he will nourish with his energy.

DR. MILLS

I know the magic there is in hope. And if I should ever forget it for even a minute, I would think again of Dr. Mills. A parishioner of mine, Dr. Sidney Mills called me frantically at eleven o'clock one night, his voice so strained I could hardly understand what he was saying. "Rabbi," he said, "my son, Steve, has been missing for five days in the Sierra Nevadas. He never came back to his campsite. Rabbi, he is only sixteen years old. The search parties say it is hopeless. Would you, as a clergyman, plead with them to search for just one more day? I don't understand why, but we need twenty-four hours. *Something inside me says tomorrow they will find him.*"

His plea was understandable, but not realistic. The search team was highly motivated and expertly trained and knew exactly how far they could reasonably go. Still, the request came from one of the warmest, most caring men I knew. I called the campsite and pleaded with the team captain "to give a miracle a chance to happen." Most of the volunteers agreed.

At four o'clock on the afternoon of the sixth day, a helicopter sighted Steve, trudging and falling, and trudging again through the snow! He was frozen, starved, and in shock—but he was alive! Later, he told us of driving his van into the woods, whereupon a heavy snow started; he had managed to turn onto an abandoned road when his wheels sank into the mud. He stayed overnight in the van and the next morning, when the snow had become a blizzard, he decided to wait it out inside the van. It lasted for three days. Afraid that he would be buried alive, he left the van and settled in a nearby cave overnight. On the sixth day, on impulse, he began to wander for hours in the white pathless expanse of the mountain wilderness. This is when he was found.

A television news chopper brought his father and me to the camp to film the reunion, and the news reporter focused on the miracle of finding Steve on that extra day. Everyone was jubilant, but baffled. The scene bore an unmistakable imprint of the supernatural. "How do you account for this, Doctor? Sheer coincidence?" the reporter asked.

"I honestly don't know. Did I somehow have an effect on the outcome? I can't say. After five days in a mountain blizzard you can't expect a person to be found alive. I truly can't make sense of it."

But as I look back on the scene today, I realize that the real miracle was not the obvious one. It was that the most logical and sober man I ever met, Dr. Mills, went beyond reason to hope. He was so convinced he was right that he kept twenty rescuers, three helicopters, and a network television crew busy for another day in frigid conditions.

It was a graphic lesson: The power of hope has little to do with reason. The strictly logical Dr. Mills hoped with passion, so passionately that he presumed it would work. *Hope moves more people to great achievements than reason does.* We can't comprehend this, because when we deal with hope, we are not dealing with science, but with spirituality. I do not understand *why* Steve was found; I *do* understand why Dr. Mills dared to hope.

> Work without hope draws nectar in a sieve
> And hope without an object cannot live.
>
> —COLERIDGE

KENNY

Kenny was one of the most affable men I ever knew. So imagine my surprise when he came to my study one day and announced he would shoot himself if I didn't give him the right answer.

"Is this a joke?" I asked him. He flew into a rage.

"Grace is pregnant. I want you, as her rabbi, to tell her that she is allowed to abort the child."

"Why would she want to do that?"

"Because I am forty-five-years old. I have three grown children, and I'm tired. All my life I wanted time to travel, enjoy, not be tied down. Now this. No. I'm not going to wait another ten years. I have a right. I earned the right. You hear me, Rabbi?"

"Does Grace want the baby?"

"Yes, but she'll agree if you give her permission."

"I will not," I said. "Listen, Kenny. You have three gifted children, each of whom you love. Now your wife is willing to bear the pain of giving birth to another. She wants this child, and she deserves it."

He glowered. Then he pulled a handgun out of his breast pocket. I was startled. He's gone berserk, I thought. He waved the gun at me, then at himself. What did he intend to do?

A moment later he put the gun back into his pocket. "I'm serious about this," he said. "Very serious. If you don't tell her to abort the baby I will leave here, get on the Ventura Freeway, and blow my brains out."

I stared at him. A kaleidoscope of pictures was whirling through my head—of blood and death and crying children and funerals and guilt. Still, I felt that no one can hold a family or a religion hostage this way. I was not responsible for this man's irrational acts, and I doubted that he would take his life over the birth of a baby.

"Kenny, if that's the way you feel, you're going to have to kill yourself," I said.

He fled my home in eye-popping rage, slammed the front door, ran to his car, and drove away.

Seven months later, during services, a note was brought to my pulpit. It read, "Please announce the birth of a baby girl to Kenny and Grace." When the service was over, Kenny was waiting for me. "It was easier to wait than to die," he said. I thanked God. I thought to myself that philosopher Friedrich Nietzsche was right after all. He once said, "What doesn't kill you, makes you stronger." In a strange way *I* became stronger, too.

Kenny had a clash of hopes. Until Grace became pregnant this last time, his hopes for his family had been realized, and the grand hope lay ahead—to have it all, and yet to be free. But some hopes must be put on hold. When Kenny said, "It was easier to wait than to die," he meant he would rather wait for that hope than take his life.

SAM

The California State Legislature passed a law permitting juries to issue verdicts of life imprisonment with no chance of parole. On hearing the news I decided to visit an inmate, Sam, a neighborhood friend I had known as a boy, who was awaiting sentencing for a very serious crime. I knew he was severely depressed, and I knew that the possibility of no parole could only deepen that feeling.

During visiting hours he asked if he could borrow my pen, which I gave him. Instantly he jabbed it into a vein in his wrist. Alarms rang, doors slammed, orderlies raced to his side. Three hours later, I was sitting at his bedside on the psychiatric floor.

During the intervening time, the prison chaplain had introduced me to two lifers who dismissed the no-parole law. They assured me that it did not mean what it said. "The law will change," one said. "They go conservative, then they go liberal." Another said, "We may have an earthquake!" I had underestimated the incredible elasticity of hope in virtually every person in virtually every condition.

After an hour of calming Sam down, I told him what the lifers had told me and that I agreed with them. Then I told him what a spokesman for the San Quentin prison said: "Wherever there's life, there's the possibility of parole." This injection of slim hope was so potent at that moment that it brought a faint smile to his face as he said, "Maybe. I *hope* so."

DO IT YOURSELF

I remember a young man sitting in my office confiding a difficult problem. After an hour's counseling, he said, "Thank you for helping. You gave me great hope. I'll have patience. I'm willing to sit and wait." I was astonished. "'Wait,' I understand. But are you going to sit around until it comes?"

This case of passive hope reminded me of a humorous story: The flooding of the Mississippi River was inundating a small Missouri community. Everyone was evacuated except for one elderly gentleman who stubbornly refused all offers of help. He climbed from the porch of his house to the roof, and prayed for God to rescue him.

When the waters rose quickly and a motorboat came to his rescue, he refused to board it. He was absolutely sure he would be saved by divine intervention. The waters rose perilously and a second boat offered help. He turned this one down, too. He was stubbornly waiting for God, in whom he trusted. When he was forced to climb still higher to the top of a nearby tree, a rescue helicopter lowered its ladder and police bullhorns pleaded with him to take hold. He declined this offer, too. "God will save me," he said. They could neither convince nor coerce him.

The river swelled and swelled and finally swallowed the bewildered man. He burst into Heaven and protested vehemently. "God, I've done so much good in my life! I trusted and I prayed and I had faith. And what did You do? Just when I needed You, You turned Your back on me!"

Instantly, a heavenly voice responded, "So why didn't you accept the offer of three messengers I sent to save you?!"

YOSEF

In Poland they tell the story of poor old Yosef, who struggled every day to earn a few kopeks gathering loose twigs and scraps of wood and selling them for firewood. He had grown too old, he moved too slowly, his back ached too much to do it anymore. "Oh, God, who needs this life?" he said, over and over. "I'm tired of it."

One day as he was gathering wood, his full sack split wide open and the lumber fell all over the cobblestones. He looked at the shambles and lamented with a head-splitting cry, "God, I told you I had enough. Take me away from this terrible place. Let me die."

At that moment, the Angel of Death appeared in front of him. "You called for me?" he said.

"Who are you?" Yosef asked.

"I am the Angel of Death," the angel said. "Can I help you?"

Yosef gulped. "Why, sure," he said after a minute. "Could you help me pick up these sticks?"

In spite of it all, our hope to live stubbornly keeps us alive.

CHAPTER SEVEN

Hoping in the Worst of Times

For me, the raison d'etre of *Camelot* was the end of the journey, when Arthur lost his love, his friend, and his Round Table, and believes his life is a failure. Then a small boy appears from behind a tent—who doesn't know the Round Table is dead, and who wishes to become a knight. Arthur realizes that as long as his vision is alive in one small heart he has not failed. Men die but an idea does not. To me, that scene was the play . . .

—ALAN JAY LERNER

S hari Lewis, the world-famous TV puppeteer (best
known for her act with her puppet Lamb Chop, as
well as for her skills, her warmth, and her talent),
has brought joy to generations of children. One very
good reason for this is the fact that she is such a joyous
person herself. She is a friend of our family. Recently
she told me about her feelings concerning hope. This is
what she said:

> For me hope is (and always has been) synonymous
> with action. As long as I *actively* attack a problem, I
> am confident that the situation can be improved, if
> not completely turned around.
>
> I was grateful for this active reflex when about a
> decade ago I was told that I had breast cancer. The doc-
> tor gravely informed me that I had to have rather
> radical surgery. Hopeful that there was another path,
> I consulted with Dr. Carl Simonton, author of *Getting
> Well Again*, and one of the earliest physicians to make
> the mind/body connection. Dr. Simonton helped me

to feel calm about my ability to explore all of the potentials and make decisions that would be right for *me*. By actively seeking other opinions, I kept hope alive long enough to find another surgeon and other treatments, and was able to avoid radical procedures and destructive chemicals. And I've been totally healthy for lo these many years!

I find that it works both ways. If you are hopeful, of *course* you can take action. The miracle occurs when you *don't* feel much hope, yet push yourself into action anyway. Perhaps it is the brain chemicals stimulated by the *action* that brings you back to hope. I don't know *why* it works. From personal experience, I just know that it *does*.

If there is one time in life when it is more difficult than another to hold on to hope, it is when we are very ill.

So with the lamps all put out, the moon sunk, and thin rain drumming on the roof, a downpouring of immense darkness began. Nothing, it seemed, could survive the flood, the profusion of darkness which, creeping in at keyholes and crevices, stole round window blinds, came into bedrooms, swallowed up here a jug and a basin, there a bowl of red and yellow dahlias, there the sharp edges and firm bulk of a chest of drawers.

The portrait of night in Virginia Woolf's *To the Lighthouse* could be a definition of terminal illness. Nothing stops it; nothing brightens the gloom. What is the use of hoping and what could we hope for anyway? After all, death is waiting at the door.

There *is* a place for hope, however, a place perhaps more important than it ever was before. Let's talk about it. Let's acknowledge that terminal illness exists, but let's talk about healing and hope.

A placebo is a substance that contains no medication but is given to patients for its psychological effect. This is what I call hope! The placebo is medicine's hope pill. Consider, for example, these familiar experiments. Two groups of subjects are given the following tests: first a symptom checklist, then a mood evaluation, and finally a personality inventory. One group is then given a placebo. In placebo testing, the effects are often noticeable at once, as anxiety and depression symptoms are markedly reduced.

In fact, the more surprising fact is that this reduction takes place as soon as the testing begins, before the placebo is even administered. Most surprising is that fully half the improvement comes before the patient is even offered a placebo at all. Obviously, virtually anything that heightens our expectations will begin our healing.

In the second experiment, the physician tells the patient that the pill he is receiving is only a placebo, but one that people have found helpful all the same. The records show that the majority who were told this believe it, and believe, too, that the pill can help them—and it *does* help them.

In the third experiment, three patients were helped enormously by a thoroughly false belief! They were told by their physician that on a certain day at three P.M. a faith healer at a distant location would perform his healing therapies on them. The healer himself was not contacted. At three P.M. all three patients reported positive feelings—feelings that lasted for some time. This tells us once again that *heightened expectations* can heal.

It is the other side of what the Harvard University *Heart Letter* has referred to as *white-coat hypertension.* The Harvard letter reported that whenever a physician, nurse, or other white-coated health professional came into the room to administer a blood-pressure test, the patient's pressure rose by 20mm in anticipation of the possibility of a high reading. This is a response to fear, just as hope is a response to the placebo.

We now know that some treatments that doctors have used throughout history were often without any medical value at all. In ages past people were bled regularly—and the sicker they got, the more they were bled. Only two generations ago, the rage was for tonsillectomies, which are now no longer considered useful except in very special cases. At the end of the nineteenth century, Oliver Wendell Holmes said that if you threw all the medicine into the sea, it would be good for mankind—but bad for fish!

Nonetheless, over the years people had witnessed enough recoveries from these procedures to retain their faith in them. Today many believe that this was simply the placebo principle at work. What this says to me is that what people *believed* to be effective helped them as much as if *it were*, in fact, an appropriate pharmaceutical.

Johns Hopkins psychiatrist Dr. Jerome Frank concludes from such studies that "Hope and positive emotions strengthen the patient's expectations of relief and are absolutely correlated with short-term improvement."

He might as well be harking back to the primary offering made by the healers of long ago—hope. With no modern medicine to guide them, the healers' aim was to arouse the patient's self-esteem, stir him emotionally, surround him with others who shared his problems (today we call that a support group), and in these ways stimulate his innate hope. The ancients understood what scientists often do not—despair only retards healing, hope only enhances it. Anxiety and despair can be lethal, confidence and hope are life-giving. Western society needs to relearn this. All of which prompts me to say once again: *No matter the prognosis, no matter the realities, always encourage a person's hope.*

To do this successfully, of course, we need to know what, under the circumstances, we should be hoping for.

Regarding that, in all my years of counseling with young and old, I have learned one vital thing about illness: People fear pain most. Even those who know that their illness is hopeless are more concerned with the pain it may cause than with anything else about it. People in pain can see no end to it.

Moreover, remember that we must differentiate between pain and suffering. Pain is a physical phenomenon that occurs when a stimulus affects the body's sensory apparatus. There can be pain without suffering, as in childbirth. And suffering alone can occur without the physical stimulus that causes pain—for example, in our suffering at the loss of a loved one. Suffering can, of course, lead to physical pain as well.

There are doctors particularly skilled in sophisticated strategies for relieving pain, although they seldom receive enough attention from health-care providers except in hospice situations. But while we may find relief from pain, we almost always find no relief from suffering. Friends or mentors or counselors may help somewhat, but in the end we ourselves need to hold fast to the hope that we can endure. I have tried to counsel parishioners, asking them to focus on the hopes that remain—that pain will be reduced, that their contributions to people will be remembered, that family conflicts will be resolved. And I prompt them to seek meaning in their suffering. These are practical considerations to hold close when it is very hard to hold anything at all.

When I am with a person who is seriously ill—or one who sees the end of the road—I watch for five hope signs. Watch for them. They will be there. They are:

- *Hope outlives the person.* Over and over I have seen it—even when a human being knows it's the end, he still harbors hope.
- *Harboring hope, he continues to believe in miracles.* Believe with that person.
- *He may now hope for a life after death,* for some immortality. This hope is not always articulated, but it is there. Believe it will happen. No one can deny it.
- *He has hopes for others—and for their futures.* He knows there will be a future, even though he may not be there to share it. Acknowledge that.
- *He hopes he will die a hero.* Heroes are found not only on battlefields, but wherever people struggle. Tell him he is one to you—it is a great solace you can offer.

Seven Hopes to Hold On To
When There Is Nothing to Hope For

૨ે

- *Hope that you will be able to cope with suffering.* This often requires an almost superhuman ability to discipline your emotions. Sometimes it helps to explore the meaning of your suffering: How has it changed you? What will the future hold? Is this period of anguish part of some overall plan you don't know about yet? Is it time to abandon some of your old goals and look for new ones?

- *Hope that something good will come from it.* Is it possible? Could you grow, could you reach another plane entirely, one you never knew existed? Perhaps you could learn who your true friends are, what is important in your daily living and what is trivial? Could you find a purpose in life you never had before?

- *Hope for remission—if not a cure.* Study the research that is being done on your condition. In modern medicine today nothing is far-fetched, the extraordinary is plausible. Don't feel foolish when you hope for a cure—it may be possible beyond your wildest expectations.

- *Hope for an extension of time.* Doctors have privately told me that they are wrong nearly 50 percent of the time in their predictions regarding survival. The strength of the mind and the power of hope together can increase your longevity. Go for it!

- *Hope for the future welfare of your family.* Pray that your spouse will manage well without you, that your children will be successful, and that the most cherished values you have imparted to them will not be lost. I advise patients to write an ethical will, one that records not only the family's inheritance, but also its heritage. This will might also be a blueprint for the family's future and an affirmation of each member's strength and how best to use it.

- *Hope to keep your dignity.* I am talking here of your inner dignity, the way you carry yourself, the way you bear your pain, the picture you leave for others to remember. Your hopes in regard to a catastrophic illness should be made manifest in a living will, which addresses the medical interventions that you wish to have employed if you are not able to articulate them at the appropriate time. Dignity is affected not by tubes and wires, but by personal bearing.

- *Hope for life after life.* For the religious person, life after we have completed this life means being welcomed into the presence of God. If you are not religious you may be more comfortable thinking of a worldly immortality—leaving behind you a good name and influencing others by deeds and actions that stay in people's memory and affect the behavior of future generations.

CHAPTER EIGHT

Ambition, Money, Hope

David Ben-Gurion, the first prime minister of modern Israel, once said that in his country if you don't believe in miracles you're not a realist!

W hen I began writing this book, I asked my good friend Alan Alda, one of the most talented and authentic men I know (and one of the wisest), what *his* hopes had been when he was young.

"Oh, mine were modest," he said. "They were strictly limited to what I thought I could achieve."

Alan is the son of Robert Alda, one of the leading stage and screen personalities of his day. Still, Alan was wise enough to realize very early that every one of us has to make it on his own; a father can be a cheering section, but he cannot make it happen for us.

And the odds of succeeding in the theater are very long indeed. Alan saw talented actors working at any job they could get to support their families. So his hopes were modest, but they absolutely never were passive—and he never abandoned them.

Alan has a ready smile. "People need an appropriate aggressiveness," he said. "You know that. And passive hope just eats you—rather than letting you take a bite out of life!

"I knew that I had to try to make something out of every chance I got. I was willing to face rejection even for the smallest things. Even for a walk-on part."

At last, of course, the big hope came true; there was *M·A·S·H*. Even with that, Alan refused to coast along in the plum role of Hawkeye. Instead he began writing, producing, and directing and stretching his artistry, honing his skills for a career that would flourish when *M·A·S·H* was finished. Needless to say, Alan Alda is a smashing success.

Someday I must ask him about the story that is still told of his father, Robert, during the latter's Hollywood days. He had been signed as a contract player at Warner Brothers, but the contract players were an anonymous lot, largely ignored by the studio executives. Sometimes, to give them something to do, it was suggested that they simply wander around the lots for a few weeks and observe the way movies were made. This is what Robert Alda did. But he also spent sleepless nights trying to think of a way to stand out among so many. He was clothes-conscious, and he decided at last to make his mark by never going to the studio in the same outfit twice. It worked. He caught people's attention, and when they were casting the role of clothes-conscious George Gershwin for the movie *Rhapsody in Blue*, he got the part.

Sometimes, to achieve what we want, we must handle

ourselves in a manner that makes it seem as if we already have it. Sometimes only the unusual works, only the outrageous makes perfect sense, and only a desperation move is the safe move to make. We can sometimes risk the unusual, the outrageous, and the desperate because we have an ultimate hope in mind.

This is particularly true, somehow, when the issue concerns money. Believe it or not, it is easier to rise above a lack of money than it is to transcend the presence of pain.

Of all human problems, the lack of money, which seems to cause the most desperation, is the most solvable. If you face a financial crisis, consider the hidden pluses in your current situation. You may not believe there are any, but take another look. Consider the case of Peter, fifty-four years old, who had been employed by the Grumman Aerospace Corporation on Long Island for twenty-nine years. At the height of production, Grumman, an aircraft and electronics systems giant, employed thousands of people. They were Big Daddy. They were Peter's security, his status, his way of life. They paid his mortgage, they put his children through school, they took care of his health. He could be impervious to any errors or sliding profits within the corporation—after all, these were *their* problems, not his. But at last everything came to a head; Grumman let thousands of those workers go. Peter was one of them. What could he do? He had four months' salary as severance pay. He could not touch his pension fund until he reached age sixty.

In chatting with Peter, what I urged him to do, before he even began planning how to use the time before him profitably, was to consider the parameters of his hopes. For example, he needed only to hope for something to do in the six years that would follow—*not* in a lifetime.

Then, *for the first time in his entire adult life*, his hopes would not be dependent on the whims of someone else: He could be his own man. In that alone there was a potential for joy that he had never experienced before.

Then too, *the second time around* he would not be simply hoping for the best. He would know he had overcome certain obstacles in life and that they were gone forever. Also, the fear, the anger, the frustration, the plain embarrassment at being dumped by the company would never haunt him again. He would be a freer man.

He decided to follow his dream. Using his engineering background, he decided to start a home-inspection business of his own, knowing the chance he took, but taking it unafraid. He knew precisely what he was hoping for and he seized the day. Peter was more alive than he ever had been!

Hopes Are No More Than Waking Dreams:
Seven Ways to Make Them Come True

ટ**ે**

- Don't look for approval of everything you do—you won't get it.
- Do, however, try to see yourself as others see you.
- Change your inner dialogue from *What's in it for me?* to *How can I help?*
- Learn from the past, set your sights on the future—but don't forget to live in the present.
- Don't constantly judge people.
- Don't look at the world around you for answers—look inside yourself instead.
- Put love in your life where fear used to be.

CHAPTER NINE

On Growing Old—
and Never Losing Hope

Scientifically, there can be no miracles. True. But science is a miracle! The thinking brain is a miracle! The feeling heart is a miracle! And hope—is hope not a miracle?

ع

On Growing Old
and Never Losing Hope

I remember visiting my parents at the Riverdale Home for the Aged, which stretches along the banks of the Hudson River in New York State. I took my father in his wheelchair up in the elevator to visit my mother, who was in the Alzheimer's pavilion. My mother was in *her* wheelchair at the window; it was the first time they had met this way, wheel to wheel. My mother was oblivious to the meeting, but my father was deeply affected. He looked at me and, without a word, turned his palms upward as his eyes filled with tears.

I knew what he was thinking: "Is this what life has come to? To such an end? Look at your mother, this lovely woman. Look at what has become of her."

I said to myself, "He's right. For what? Is this his reward? For the thousand smiles he brought to strangers' faces, for the heartiness he brought to every gathering, for all the energy he expended working at three jobs to support his family until he was eighty, enduring hardships from employers not worth his shoe leather? Now he doesn't have the strength to walk a hundred feet to see the wife he loves. For what? Is this all there is?

"He can hardly see, she can hardly recognize. He can't read; she can't understand. He lost his patience; she lost her mind. For what?"

Despair wins.

I went to the window to give them a few moments alone, moments to gaze at each other and to hold hands. I stood looking out on the landscape below. The sun warmed my face. I studied the horizon, where the blue sky met the stone pillars of the Jersey Palisades, then gazed down at the Hudson River, and then at the smooth green lawns of the home.

On that Sunday afternoon, a flock of grandchildren were romping, running around the old folks who were gathered there. At the far end, teenage lovers chased one another around a large maple—eyes wild with the eternal chase.

Just under my window was a boy about three years old, wearing a baseball cap cocked to one side. He looked up at me and smiled. He waved, and I returned the wave. He laughed heartily at that, and I laughed with him. Then he called two little friends, pointed up to my window, and they all laughed, and I laughed, and they all waved at me. And I looked hard and I breathed a deep breath and I squeezed that sight behind my closed eyes, committing it to memory, and inside my chest I felt a slow spreading of warmth, and calm, and I knew.

Hope wins.

Old age is not a disease. You would never discover this from our vocabulary, which shuns the word "old" and disguises it with such terms as "senior years," "modern maturity," or "golden years."

It is true that when we grow into old age, our strength sags, our inhibitions often are shed, our interests change, and long-repressed personality traits—some good, some not so nice—sharpen. But none of this necessarily means that we are going to vanish right away—we are *here*!

D. H. Lawrence, in *Sons and Lovers*, describes the crumbling of a multicolored sunset:

> The gold clouds fall to pieces, and go in immense, rose-colored ruin toward the darkness. Gold flamed to scarlet, like pain in intense brightness. Then the scarlet ran to rose, and rose to crimson, and quickly the passion went out of the sky. All the world was dark gray.

I do not believe the passion has to go out of our sky in late afternoon! Twilights do not all have to be dark gray! Can we not paint crimson on the muted tones of dusk? Doesn't our intelligence, our will, our humanity, make any difference in how we spend those twilight years?

Can we not devise a way to hold back our slide into the darkness? "Rage, rage against the dying of the light," Dylan Thomas said to his father.

People don't rage; sometimes they simply submit and act according to the script. My wife Shirley hears hope after hope dashed every day on the hotline for the National Institute for Jewish Hospice. An elderly terminally ill man asked his daughter to buy him a tube of toothpaste, and she bought him one—the smallest size the manufacturer makes. "Look at this," he said, holding it up in the air. "That's how long she thinks I'll last!" Visitors bring flowers that will die overnight, instead of plants that will put forth new shoots and bloom again. They offer this excuse: "It will last longer than she will."

There is a song from the past that may come back to haunt us—"When I Grow Too Old to Dream." It's a nice song, but it's not true. We *never* grow too old to dream—some dream. Our dreams change, that's all. Hopes which can hold back the dying of the light can come in a potted plant, in a giant-sized tube of toothpaste.

Regenerating our hope often requires an explicit, conscious effort—especially when it looks like it's slipping away in the twilight of our lives. We have spent all our lives in hope, and we should not be willing to surrender so easily.

From the day we are born until the day we die we need hope. An infant hopes to be fed, a child to be loved, a teenager to be popular, a college student to succeed. Because life is unthinkable without such hopes, we never *do* think about them. Modern medicine has devised means to define inner processes with which we have lived all our lives without understanding them.

For the past thirty years biofeedback has been in use to help us to understand why we behave the way we do. This knowledge is power. Psychologists believe that this awareness of our inner behavior patterns helps us to control them. The same is true of hope. Repeating anything continuously, *without thinking* about it—even a hope—is like knitting while watching television: We are concentrating on the screen, not the knitting. We are not *consciously* hoping when we dull our hopes by *thoughtless* repetition.

Maybe that is why we fail to realize that, as we grow older, hopes don't die (or they shouldn't) but they change (*and they should*).

If you are young as you are reading this, stop and think for a moment of the hopes and dreams that still seem to lie so far ahead. If you are no longer young, the time may have come for you to seize them—they are your passport to the future. *But no matter your age, you must have hopes.* Sometimes they may sound like new verses to an old melody—that doesn't matter. *The song is still playing for you.* Here are a few hopes you may acquire as time goes by; take them and hold them close for the rest of your life.

A Creed for the Later Years

&.

- I hope I will always appreciate new thoughts, new ideas, and the life of the mind.
- I hope I will always take time to listen to the opinions of others.
- I hope I will not stop exploring the best of everything in a changing world.
- I hope I will be called wise but not opinionated.
- I hope I will be considered a person of innate dignity and not a prude.
- I hope that all I have learned along the way will not go to waste.
- I hope I will remember when I am slowing down that it wasn't easy being young.
- I hope I will like myself a lot—*just as I am.*
- I hope my grown children and my grandchildren will be, above all else, my best friends.
- I hope I am never too old to change—my home, my activities, my priorities, my point of view.
- I hope I will never call my time limited, but instead realize that it is its quality, not its quantity, that counts.
- I hope I can laugh—*at least* once every day.

CHAPTER TEN

I Will Take You Through the Darkest Nights—to the Brightest Days—and We Will Defeat Hopelessness Together

The founder of a museum which memorializes the tenement life of old New York says that the telling quality of the residents of those multiracial, multicultural tenements was that "common to all is that they kept their vision, even in the dark."

ᔐ

I am going to take you all the way to the spot where hope shines brightest. But don't think I am unaware that there will be low points in our travels, points when you feel you are walking through a dark night with nothing but more darkness ahead, when you become convinced that you have been living on illusions, when you believe there is no hope at all—and whatever made you think there was?

I'm sure that this has happened to you in the past; it will happen again. When it does, the smallest thing becomes insurmountable. Sometimes this kind of depression is triggered by something insignificant in itself—an argument with a spouse, a disappointment in a child, a lovers' quarrel, even a victory that turns out to be hollow. (But don't forget, "happily ever after" is a mirage. "Happily," yes; "ever after," no.)

Hopelessness is poison and it is infectious; if it festers, it will be fatal. But you can beat it—it is not a natural condition. Survival is natural, and so is change. When I was a freshman at college, I was sure that nothing could stand in the way of my destined success. Then I discovered such exotic obstacles as money and people—and even some personal inadequacies. This was not total failure, but it was a loss of hope. The good news is that the world of hope has a very efficient lost-and-found system. Whatever is lost can be replaced—even if the single specific hope that is lost will never be found again. We substitute, often instantaneously, new hopes for old.

Adults usually lose hope following the collapse of one pivotal, meaningful desire that has stood at the vortex of a lifetime of yearning—if we suddenly realize that we are not qualified to perform as we always had expected we would; if we suffer a severe economic loss that seems irreparable; if we feel abandoned; if we are devastated by a force of nature. A woman whose husband has left her and who has no resources will cry out, "There's nothing left for me. Look what happened to my life!" The home of an elderly couple is ravaged by a flood. They have no insurance and in a flash they are penniless and homeless. Such people are severely depleted and many become convinced that they are fated to be losers—but it isn't so.

In only very rare instances does the failure of hope strike with such catastrophic force that it paralyzes its victim, rendering him totally helpless. Such a wound is pathological and requires professional intervention. On the other hand, if you are reading this book about hope, you have already shown that you are willing to engage in a search for hope—and therefore you are *not* hopeless!

Some years ago a group of scientists conducted experiments involving survival tactics among certain species. First they placed frogs in a basin filled with water, then heated the water gradually until it reached a temperature that would be fatal to the frogs. They observed that the frogs sat in the water slowly cooking and did not move until it was too late to jump out and save themselves. Next they studied chickens when a hawk attacks them. They found that at the moment of attack the chicken freezes rather than fleeing for cover, and that it remains frozen for minutes—or even hours. In other words, both respond by succumbing—because they are convinced they cannot escape. But we are civilized human beings—not frogs and not chickens. We need to jump out of hot water and we need to run to safety—we shouldn't succumb to suffer from passivity. When the world is too much with us, though, we may need some help in fighting back, with some quick solutions that are close at hand. Here are seven of them to use as you see fit.

Seven Mind Turners

❧

- *Change the atmosphere around you.* If fear comes in the dark of night, put the lights on. If it wakes you from sleep, get out of bed, go somewhere else in the house. If you are warm, open a window and feel the breeze. If the silence is deadly, turn on the radio. If loneliness haunts you, telephone a friend. If you can possibly leave the premises entirely, do so. You may discover that, to find hope, you have to go looking!

- *When life is not a song, sing anyway!* You don't need to be Pavarotti or Beverly Sills. Just open up, let your song fill the air, sing on even though no one can hear you. You cannot imagine how this will set you free. Once I had a very buoyant friend, Ludwig Lipmann. Ludwig was stricken with cancer. One day in his oncologist's waiting room (one of the sadder places on earth), he looked around at other patients who obviously were facing what he was facing. All at once he lifted his head and began to sing quietly.

  The lady next to him paused for a moment, smiled, then began to hum the tune of his song. A little girl and her mother soon did the same, then an elderly black man who had just come into the room. The nurse, trained in the rules of silence in a doctor's office, walked over to quiet Ludwig, but by this time everyone was singing or humming. The doctor, hearing the noise, came in to see what had happened. Ludwig sang to him, directly from the Book of Psalms: *I will lift up my eyes to the mountains from where will come my help. My help comes from the Lord, Creator of Heaven and Earth.*

The doctor crossed the room, sat down, and sang along with his patients.

- *Dance the night away.* Try it. Dance all alone in your living room in the middle of the night if you must, and note when you do how soothing the movement is—how easy it is to feel you are dancing to the beat of a higher drummer. After all, when writers refer to the dance of life they are describing liquid in motion, a life uninterrupted and unperturbed by the jagged, irrational troubles of the outside world. Look at your face in the mirror when you are dancing. Don't be surprised if it is radiant. Nothing can hurt you while you dance—it can make you smile all by yourself. And although you can dance alone perfectly well, remember that most dancing is sharing. It means touching, connecting with another human being. Feelings of hopelessness drop away when we no longer feel alone.

- *At long last, laugh!* Victor Borge is fond of saying that laughter is the shortest distance between two people. Norman Cousins once estimated that one hour of comedy equals two hours of good sleep. Don't think that laughter is frivolous, or that you don't deserve it, or that life is too somber to tolerate it. You might even save some special laughter for a rainy day. Tape some comedy routines you like, keep books written by your favorite humorists on your night table for dipping into at bad times, put a warm and funny picture of somebody you love on the bulletin board in your kitchen. Keep laughter close at hand and it will be there when you need it.

- *Look better—life will look better too.*

> Give me my scallop-shell of quiet,
> My staff of faith to walk upon.
> My scrip of joy, immortal diet,
> My bottle of salvation,
> My gown of glory, hope's true gauge,
> And thus I'll take my pilgrimage.

This fragment from a poem by Sir Walter Raleigh was incorporated by Caroline Kennedy Schlossberg and John F. Kennedy, Jr. into the funeral service of their mother, Jacqueline Kennedy Onassis. More than many of her contemporaries, Jacqueline Onassis had understood the special role that appearance plays at various times in our lives and the power it has to make things happen. This was true whether she was dazzling de Gaulle in her Givenchy in Paris, bringing hats into favor by wearing a pillbox, or standing in starkest black, a veil shrouding her features, on a hillside in Arlington National Cemetery. It was evident to her family that, on her greatest pilgrimage, she would undoubtedly wear nothing but a "gown of glory."

So should we. It is not a question of originals, or fashions, or fads. It has to do with caring about ourselves and the image of ourselves we want the world to see. The better that image is, the better we look to others, the better we feel inside and the more confident we will be that we can do nothing wrong. There are good reasons to pamper yourself, perfect your makeup, buy that new lipstick, highlight your hair, maintain your wardrobe, walk like a winner. The world will only judge you by what they can see—and when you walk with beauty, you walk with hope as well. When you are feeling lowest, wrap yourself in the most beautiful colors you can find and just feel your spirit glow.

- *Say to yourself at least once each week: "Tell how it's gonna be, George."* In John Steinbeck's novel *Of Mice and Men*, he portrayed Lennie, a slow-witted man who is totally dependent upon his companion, George. At the end of every day, Lennie makes the same request. "Tell how it's gonna be, George," he says. And every day George paints the future for him: the farm they will own, the fields that will belong to them— always the same, always repeated in the same way.

Steinbeck himself said that Lennie represented the inarticulate and powerful yearning of all men . . . a study of the dreams and pleasures of everyone in the world. He was right. We all need reassurance about the future and we need it every day. When your dreams seem to be shattered, ask a spouse, a parent, a friend you can trust, to help you put them back together again. Ask them to tell you how it's gonna be.

- *Tell God all about it.* Some people have lived their entire lives without ever talking to God—often because they do not even know how to start. It's easy; here's how:

  - Talk in your own language, the way you would to a friend.
  - Do this when no one else is around to hear.
  - Don't feel guilty for neglecting to do it up to now. He has been waiting to hear from you and He is delighted!
  - If it's hard at first, keep trying. Practice makes perfect.
  - Ask for His help—that is what He's there for.
  - Tell Him everything. You may not realize this, but He knows it all anyway.

All of these steps will lead you into the morning and out of the shadows. Hopelessness will become unthinkable.

CHAPTER ELEVEN

Hope Therapy

One of the magical qualities of hope is its ability to silently reformulate itself to adapt to changing conditions. It defies logic; presses for life when life is impossible; turns us to the future when we are tempted to stop and wrestle with the past, and then moves us to begin that future. It makes us talk success in the presence of fear; encourages us to leap over obstacles; enables us to recoup it after we lose it; and then miraculously adjusts itself to suit our every change!

❧

The Ten-Point Plan
That Can Turn Hope into Reality

❧

By now I hope you know what hope is and I hope you understand the incredible things it can accomplish. You understand it, you are not afraid of it, you know how to handle it, and you want to make it work for you. I promised to show you how to do that, and I will. This is the formula. I have used it in my own family and in my years of counseling others. It works. It is not a dream; it is not a flight of fancy. It is a ten-point program that will lead you where you want to go. Let's look at it.

- *Find a trust person.* People need people. A trust person is someone you have great faith in. It might be an old friend, a mentor, an office colleague, a relative. You must choose your trust person with the greatest care. He must be able to do four things: put himself in your place, tell you the truth as he sees it, advise you without being judgmental, and be reliable. Let me advise you here that the people you love the most are often *not* ideal for this role—they can be too close to be dispassionate.

  A sensitive person will know right away when to be a sounding board. He will see at once how impor-

tant his role is going to be—instinctively he is someone who understands the satisfaction of shared hopes.
The very vulnerability you show in asking him to
help can lead to a strong bonding between the two of
you and the beginning of a deep friendship. Kahlil
Gibran, the poet-philosopher, observed that we may
forget people whom we have laughed with, but we
never forget those who share our crying.

  If, after taking all this into consideration, you
absolutely cannot think of an ideal person for this
role, you *can* do it alone—it will simply take more
self-discipline and more determination. If you are persistent, however, you will succeed.

• *Find a place for reflection that is all your own, and a
  time that is yours alone, too.* I call the hideaway you
  need the mulling corner, as the writer Lewis Mumford
  called it. It should be private. Ideally, it should contain
  a comfortable chair and a desk or table for writing any
  notes you may take. If there is no room in your home,
  though, even your car will serve—or perhaps your
  office is a place where you can be alone. Set your
  alarm to remind you of your mulling time and note it
  on your calendar—this is a regular appointment that
  you will keep every day. Never feel you are too busy
  for it and *never* apologize to others for this period of
  withdrawal. What is more important than creating
  your future? Think of all the games you have seen on
  television when time-out is called so that players can

discuss strategy—that's what you are doing. In your mulling corner you will close your eyes and trace in your mind what lies ahead. Or what *should* lie ahead.

- *Learn how to let go.* It may surprise you to know that there are things you should not hope for anymore. Some things we hope for all our lives—and we shouldn't. Of course, some hopes you can go along with and keep alive. Every time you fall in love, you hope it will last forever. When you have good health, if you give it any thought, you hope you never will be sick. Each year, you hope for the perfect vacation. Keep doing that.

The hopes that are like excess baggage are the ones to shed. They are dated, they are failed, they are as far off now as they were when you first had them. Whenever you have been waiting an inordinately long time for something to happen and it has not, it is time to wonder about it.

But for some hopes you need to learn to wait. To know how to wait is to be the tiger at the edge of the rock. Long before he sees his prey he crouches, tensing his body, building up his kinetic energy, digging in his paws, waiting to leap. When he sights an animal he is ready—he springs and seizes it. This can be applied to daily living. The best way to get the job of your dreams is to apply for another one. When you have taken a test, don't wait for the mark you will receive—

study instead for the next test. A wise man once said, "Hope is the passion for the possible."

There is the old story of Daniel, who, very upset, called his friend David. "David," he said, "I can see God looking at me through my office window. What should I do?"

"Look busy," David said. "Look busy!"

Learning how to let go is harder than waiting. It is easier to hang on to old dreams than it is to give them up. But that is self-defeating. It is easier to hope for the impossible than to face reality—but we have to live in the real world. Only when we give up what is hopeless do we begin to heal and does the future begin to take shape.

- *Refuse to be a victim.* You will find, if you have not already, that life is a battlefield—and a battlefield must have its winners and its losers. Invariably there are going to come times when you are one of the latter, but let me warn you of one thing. Be a loser if you must, *but don't be a victim!* Victims don't give, they always receive. People who give have power. To rise from our losses we need to be heroic—to be confident and to give others courage. When you do that, you become a star. This is no mere survival; it is beyond that. If you can, as you regroup your forces, give by providing active encouragement to others. Reverse the flow—don't become a collector of sympathy, become a contributor of positive thoughts, of personal strength, of hope. You will reach a level of stardom that will give you deep satisfaction.

No matter what, *don't make sympathy a way of life*. The most well-meaning people in the world have a low threshold for sustaining compassion for others; they develop what I have termed "compassion fatigue." When people begin referring to you as "that poor thing," then you have become a victim. You are a thing, an object, not a person. You have convinced those around you that you can't handle life by yourself. That is the path to hopelessness.

And here is how to avoid it: Confide in your trust person and perhaps in one other whom you are close to—a sibling, a parent, a child—someone who will understand your misfortune and may be in a position to help and *will not talk to others about it*. Even when you share these confidences, keep them mercifully brief and make it very clear that you are looking for advice and not for compassion. And, no matter how sad your story, *always* end it on a note of hope. Tomorrow has to be better—assure your confidant that you feel this way.

- *Take a first step*. Very early in your program of hope, do something, even if it is only a single thing, to bring yourself a step closer to fulfilling your heart's desire. If you don't, it may remain far off in a dream state— and you will never get any closer to it than that. Let me give you an example; let me tell you about

John Ausland. John was a bright young man with high hopes but no job, and a single ambition—he wanted to be an advertising artist. There was a recession on, however. Large corporations were downsizing jobs in this field and his prospects were growing more lean and mean every day.

John did not let this stop him. He took action. He focused on a small design agency called Wild Dog. First he tried to get an interview. No luck. Then he triggered his imagination.

He bought a doorman's cap and stationed himself at the entrance of the building where Wild Dog had its offices. For several days every morning he handed a copy of the *Wall Street Journal* to the president of Wild Dog when he arrived. He followed this up with drawings he sent anonymously to the agency. John had tailored them to fit a campaign he had heard the agency was undertaking. The next time he saw the president he mentioned the drawings (still anonymous) and asked if he had seen them. This prompted the president to dig them out of his attaché case. He found them young, innovative, and fresh—he wanted to meet the artist who had drawn them. John was hired, and seven months later he became the creative director of the Wild Dog Agency—the youngest man ever to hold the office.

The first step starts you off. *Then hope, once activated, develops a propensity for perpetual motion.*

- *Look ahead; it's not the end.* Never lose faith in your-self. Remember what we said about fear. Franklin Delano Roosevelt put hope in the hearts of a terrified nation swamped by the Depression with the simple words, "The only thing we have to fear is fear itself."

  It may look like the end right now. But there are fewer endings than you think. The end of a job is *not* the end of joy. The end of marriage is *not* the end of hope. And the end of life itself is a foyer to the here-after. If you think you are lost, you are. Carry on. Hope on. Echo the Italian patriot Garibaldi, who told his troops on the eve of combat, "I cannot promise you victory, I can only assure you a great battle!"

- *Find the proper goal to hope for.* Every one of us has the right to hope and the need to dream. Our hopes are stepping-stones toward the far pavilion we may have been reaching for since childhood. Don't give up now. Do, however, give some thought to it. Sit in your mulling corner, lean back, close your eyes, and ask yourself if the person you are today really wants the wishes of yesterday to come true. Try this test: Imag-ine trying to plant an orchard—without seeds. The wind and the sun will do nothing for it; the rain will make only mud. To get growth you need the potential. Does the grand design you have in mind for the you of tomorrow have roots in the you of today? If it doesn't, now is the time to find that out—and to search for the hope that will enable you to grow into your future, based on what you have accomplished in your past. That *is* right for you at this moment.

- *Don't let anyone take any hope away from you.* They can't—unless you let them. Sometimes, the most well-meaning friends work very hard at destroying your hopes. Their motives are often the best. They don't want to see you hurt. They see the dark side of your dream; they see the failure, the frustration that could lie ahead. They present every negative argument they know—and they are people you trust, so you listen. They may be your parents, a doctor, a college professor, a business associate. They frighten you. There is only one solution: When you see them coming, *run*!

- *Make trouble work for you.* I spoke earlier of adversity, but it is such a vital part of your program that I must repeat it. The acknowledgment of failure can never be very far from the hope for success. And, after all, history begins with adversity—as told to us in the Book of Genesis. When Adam and Eve were expelled from the Garden of Eden, they went east of Eden. In exile, life changed for them. They had to labor hard for their daily bread, rather than pluck ready-to-eat food from burgeoning trees as they had done before. In paradise everything was free, thanks to the good Lord. East of Eden offered no free lunch—or breakfast or dinner. They worked by the sweat of their brows; they struggled through thorns and thistles. But here's the stunning miracle of humanity: Only then did they become creative, productive, and thoughtful. And only then did they have children, build a family, erect a home, and begin a civilization. We live east of Eden. Our world is not a paradise. What we need for personal satisfaction and a sense of self-worth is work more than rest, creativity more than comfort. We grow by exertion, not by endowment.

And should we hit bottom, we have no choice but to look around, see things as they are, and start climbing up again. In that process, we will learn at least one thing: *When you can't change conditions around you, you must change yourself.* This is the time when you *know* you must drop all the old futile hopes and the implausible fantasies and substitute new ones that will work. Don't forget your adversity—it's too useful to abandon.

The Chinese have a single symbol that stands for both danger and opportunity. Every danger, they believe, has a rare opportunity hidden inside. And every new opportunity has danger at its core. So not only can adversity clear the air—it can give you a whole new start.

- *After you have tried, trust.* This is the final step, and it is, in many ways, the most important. After you have tried your best, you must *believe* that your goals will be accomplished. And you must never lose faith. This is faith in its grandest sense, meaning simply that you feel *confident* that something specific will happen—the rains that are destroying your crops will end, you will reach an understanding with your wife and save your marriage, your son will make the right decision regarding his career. This confidence is strengthened by your faith in God, or in a Higher Power. When we have that, we are secure, because we trust in a Providence who has the power to intervene in the affairs of the world and take care of us. Most of us, knowing this, have no fear of fear.

Most of us are spiritually attuned, whether we are formally religious or not, and our souls need to go beyond *trying* to be trusting—in God, in a transcendent force, in a Higher Power that determines our destinies. We can't trust in trying alone.

No one sails through life on a serene sea, oars shipped, with a gentle breeze at our backs. We experience, at some time in our lives—if not more often—a severe loss of hope, a numbness in the face of a staggering problem, disappointment in ourselves. We may at this moment be wrestling with an intractable dilemma. We search for some solution, a key, a way out, a glimmer of good news. How will we manage, after we have exhausted our resources and yet remain in a gum of troubles from which we cannot free ourselves?

We turn to God. We place our hopes on God's shoulders. Some do this because they think of God as a partner in life, and have a running conversation with Him about the major happenings of their lives. Many wonderful people who do not subscribe to any formal religion do just that.

There lingers inside all of us a ray—a single stray beam—which diffuses our souls, our hopes, with a faint glow. "Maybe. Just maybe."

But now I urge you to take that final step. After you

have tried your best, you need to *trust* that your goals will be accomplished.

So take my hand. We have come a long way together. We will go all the way together.